The Dispeller of Disputes

The Dispeller of Disputes

Nāgārjuna's *Vigrahavyāvartanī*

Translation and Commentary by

JAN WESTERHOFF

OXFORD
UNIVERSITY PRESS

2010

OXFORD
UNIVERSITY PRESS

Oxford University Press, Inc., publishes works that further
Oxford University's objective of excellence
in research, scholarship, and education.

Oxford New York
Auckland Cape Town Dar es Salaam Hong Kong Karachi
Kuala Lumpur Madrid Melbourne Mexico City Nairobi
New Delhi Shanghai Taipei Toronto

With offices in
Argentina Austria Brazil Chile Czech Republic France Greece
Guatemala Hungary Italy Japan Poland Portugal Singapore
South Korea Switzerland Thailand Turkey Ukraine Vietnam

Published by Oxford University Press, Inc.
198 Madison Avenue, New York, New York 10016

www.oup.com

Library of Congress Cataloging-in-Publication Data
Nāgārjuna, 2nd cent.
[Vigrahavyāvartanī. English]
The dispeller of disputes : Nāgārjuna's Vigrahavyāvartanī / Jan Westerhoff.
p. cm.
Translation and commentry by Jan Westerhoff.
Includes bibliographical references.
ISBN 978-0-19-973269-2; 978-0-19-973270-8 (pbk.)
1. Madhyamika (Buddhism)—Early works to 1800.
I. Westerhoff, Jan. II. Title.
BQ2902.E5 2010
294.3'85—dc22 2009023180

Printed in the United States of America
on acid-free paper

To the best of speakers

Acknowledgments

I would like to thank the following for their most helpful advice, pertaining to matters of both philosophy and philology: Kamaleswar Bhattacharya, Jonardon Ganeri, Jay Garfield, Jowita Kramer, David Seyfort Ruegg, Mattia Salvini, and Mark Siderits.

Contents

The Dispeller of Disputes

I

Introduction

There is no doubt that this treatise of Nāgārjuna
needs to have a wider philosophic audience.

—Matilal 1987: 187

Given the rising interest in Madhyamaka philosophy in the recent past, this remark by Bimal Matilal is even more true today than it was over twenty years ago. In fact, "The Dispeller of Disputes," the *Vigrahavyāvartanī*, is an ideal companion piece to Nāgārjuna's main philosophical treatise, the *Mūlamadhyamakakārikā* or "Fundamental Verses on the Middle Way." It covers some important topics that do not play a big role in this larger work (such as epistemology and the philosophy of language), and it does so in an unusual question-and-answer format. In the *Vigrahavyāvartanī* we find Nāgārjuna replying to a series of specific objections against his theory of universal emptiness that are raised by both Buddhist and non-Buddhist scholars. As such, the text is obviously of historical interest, as it gives us an insight into the kind of philosophical debates conducted in ancient India in the early days of Madhyamaka thought during the first and second centuries CE. Moreover, and perhaps more important, the *Vigrahavyāvartanī* is also a tremendously interesting philosophical work. Many key questions and objections that occur to the reader of Nāgārjuna's philosophical texts are set out and discussed in this work, which allows us to gain a view of a variety of additional facets of the core theory of Madhyamaka. For those who regard Nāgārjuna's Madhyamaka as a philosophical system that not only was historically very influential but also has a considerable systematic appeal, the discussion contained in the *Vigrahavyāvartanī* is an invaluable resource.

History of the Text

The *Vigrahavyāvartanī* consists of seventy verses in Āryā meter together with an autocommentary in prose following each verse. The text is divided into two parts: the first twenty verses (together with the commentary, this is just under a third of the entire text) present a set of criticisms of Nāgārjuna's theory of universal emptiness. In the second part, Nāgārjuna spends the remaining fifty verses replying to these objections.

Even though the *Vigrahavyāvartanī* was composed in Sanskrit, prior to 1937 no Sanskrit version of the text was available. The first translations into Western languages were based on Tibetan and Chinese translations of the original Sanskrit. An edition of the Tibetan text based on the versions found in the sNar thang and Peking bsTan 'gyur was published by Giuseppe Tucci in 1929.[1] The Tibetan translation of the verses was made in 842 CE by Jñānagarbha and later revised by the Kashmiri Jayānanda and the Tibetan mDo sde dpal in 1060 CE. Jñānagarbha and Ban de rakṣita translated the commentary.[2]

The Chinese translation is considerably earlier; it was translated by Vimokṣa Prajñāṛṣi together with Gautama Prajñāruci in 541 CE.[3] Susumu Yamaguchi published a French translation of the Tibetan version in the *Journal Asiatique* of 1929. In the same year, Giuseppe Tucci brought out his *Pre-Diṅnāga Texts on Logic from Chinese Sources*, which contains an English translation of the Chinese translation. On the whole, the Tibetan translation appears to give a more precise and philosophically accurate rendering of the *Vigrahavyāvartanī* than the Chinese. Fortunately, contemporary scholars, unlike Yamaguchi and Tucci, do not have to rely exclusively on either of these translations any more.

On 28 July 1936, the Indian scholar Rāhula Sāṇkṛtyāyana discovered a manuscript of the Sanskrit version of the *Vigrahavyāvartanī* in a bundle of thirty-nine other Sanskrit texts at Zhwa lu ri phug, a hermitage-like retreat behind the monastery of Zhwa lu in midwestern Tibet.[4] The manuscript

1. A new edition encorporating the sDe dge and Co ne versions as well is given in Yonezawa (2008).

2. Sāṇkṛtyāyana (1937: viii).

3. Taishō volume 32, number 1631, a newly revised version is in Miyamoto (1999). See also Yamaguchi (1949).

4. His four expeditions to Tibet in search of Sanskrit mansucripts between the years 1929 and 1938 are described in Sāṇkṛtyāyana (1935; 1937; 1938). For the visit to Zhwa lu, see Sāṇkṛtyāyana (1937: 9–15). See also Steinkellner (2004: 11–17).

consists of seven palm leaves inscribed in Tibetan *dBu med* script. In 1961, the manuscript was brought to Beijing and later returned to Lhasa, where it is now kept in the Tibet Museum.[5]

The colophon mentions that it was copied by a scribe named Dharmakīrti. Another text from the same bundle from the hand of the same copyist informs us that it was written down in India while Dharmakīrti stayed at the monastery of Vikramaśilā (in present-day Bihar). The manuscript is not dated, but from a number of incidental clues Sāṇkṛtyāyana infers that it was probably written sometime between 1100 and 1120 CE (about a thousand years after the composition of the *Vigrahavyāvartanī*).[6] Recent research by Yoshiasu Yonezawa suggests a date somewhere between 1090 and 1125.[7]

The first edition of this manuscript, based on a handwritten copy made at Zhwa lu (unlike others, the manuscript was not photographed at the time), was published in 1937 by Sāṇkṛtyāyana. This appeared as an appendix to the *Journal of the Bihar and Orissa Research Society*; it is essentially a copy of the Sanskrit text with very little change, even though it does take account of the Tibetan translation.[8]

The most useable edition of the Sanskrit is one prepared by Elgin H. Johnston and Arnold Kunst up to the former's death in 1942 and published in the *Mélanges chinois et bouddhiques* in 1947.[9] The great advantage of this edition is that it tries to improve on the readings of the Sanskrit manuscript, which, unfortunately, is not in very good shape. Though complete, it contains a large number of omissions, additions, and other mistakes. Johnston and Kunst used the Sāṇkṛtyāyana edition as the basic text and employed the Tibetan translation in order to reconstruct the Sanskrit text that the Tibetan translators had in front on them. Cases of disagreement between the Sanskrit and Tibetan text have been decided by appeal to the Chinese translation.[10] Johnston and Kunst succeeded admirably in producing a version of the Sanskrit text "which is readable and as close to the original as the material permits."[11]

Even though this edition has become the standard resource for scholars, it contains a variety of philological problems. The most important of these is

5. Steinkellner (2004: 20–21), Yonezawa (2008: 211).

6. Sāṇkṛtyāyana (1937: viii–ix).

7. Hiraga et al. (2001: 8).

8. Sāṇkṛtyāyana's rendering of the Sanskrit manuscript is not always faithful, though. See Yonezawa (1991).

9. This is now most easily available as a reprint in Bhattacharya et al. (1978).

10. The most important of the rare cases where the Chinese has been followed even though the Sanskrit and Tibetan agree on a different reading is the final portion of verse 20. Both say "therefore substance does not exist" (*yataḥ svabhāvo 'san, rang bzhin yod min*), as it is the opponent speaking; however, it is evident that we should read with the Chinese "therefore substance exists".

11. Bhattacharya et al. (1978: 36).

that Johnston and Kunst had no access to the Sanskrit manuscript itself but had to work with Sāṇkṛtyāyana's *editio princeps*, which is not always accurate in its rendering of the manuscript. Moreover, the Tibetan text used in their reconstructions is Tucci's edition, which only uses two of the available versions.

It is therefore very fortunate that in 2001 Taishō University published a facsimile edition of a collection of Sanskrit manuscripts including the *Vigrahavyāvartanī*.[12] Even more useful is a transliteration of the Sanskrit manuscript published by Yonezawa in 2008, which in addition provides an edition of the Tibetan text based on four different versions. The translation of the *Vigrahavyāvartanī* provided here is based on the Sanskrit text edited by Yonezawa. Where this Sanskrit text is defective, however, I follow the Tibetan translation, which I also do in some instances where it appears to provide a philosophically more interesting reading.

The Question of Authenticity

The *Vigrahavyāvartanī* belongs to a group of six works known as the Yukti-corpus (the Tibetan tradition refers to it as the "collection of the six texts on reasoning" (*rigs pa'i tshogs drug*). Apart from the *Mūlamadhyamakakārikā* and the *Vigrahavyāvartanī*, this set of Nāgārjuna's core philosophical works contains the "Sixty Stanzas on Reasoning" (*Yuktiṣaṣṭikā*), the "Seventy Stanzas on Emptiness" (*Śūnyatāsaptati*), the "Treatise on Pulverization" (*Vaidalyaprakaraṇa*), and the "Precious Garland" (*Ratnāvalī*).[13] The colophons of the Sanskrit manuscript, and of the Chinese and the Tibetan translation ascribe the *Vigrahavyāvartanī* to Nāgārjuna, as do a variety of Madhyamaka authors quoting it, such as Bhāviveka, Candrakīrti, and Śāntarakṣita.[14] It has to be borne in mind, however, that the authors of the colophons, the scribe Dharmakīrti, and the translators, as well as the later commentators, are separated from Nāgārjuna by several centuries, a fact that makes their attributions sometimes less certain than we would hope them to be. This is particularly true in the light of the vast quantity of very different works that have been traditionally ascribed to Nāgārjuna, twenty-four in the Chinese and as many as 123 in the Tibetan canon. Modern scholars have

12. Hiraga et al. (2001).

13. In some lists the *Ratnāvalī* is replaced by the no longer extant *∗Vyavahārasiddhi*. See Ruegg 1981: 8.

14. Lindtner (1982a: 70, notes 101–104). If we follow Ruegg (1981: 61) in dating Bhāviveka to 500–570, it is evident that Yonezawa (2008: 209, note 1) is mistaken in claiming that in Indian sources "no reference to the *Vigrahavyāvartanī* is traceable before Candrakīrti (ca. 600–650 A.D.)." This of course only holds if the Bhāviveka or Bhavya who wrote the *∗Madhyamakaratnapradīpa* (which contains the attribution in question) is identical with the author of the *Prajñāpradīpa* and is not a later author of the same name. On this matter see Ruegg (1981: 66–67, note 214), Hiraga et al. (2001: 25, note 3).

attempted to categorize these in terms of their possible authenticity. Lindtner lists thirteen works as "genuine," including all the works in the Yukti-corpus.[15] Other major Madhyamaka scholars such as David Seyfort Ruegg (as well as all the translators and editors of the text) also regard the *Vigrahavyāvartanī* as a work of Nāgārjuna.[16]

The most detailed case against attributing the *Vigrahavyāvartanī* to Nāgārjuna has been made by Fernando Tola and Carmen Dragonetti in a paper published in 1998. Their argument focuses on two main issues. First, they note the relatively close similarity between the *Vigrahavyāvartanī* and the *Vaidalyaprakaraṇa*, a discussion of the categories of the Nyāya school only preseved in Tibetan translation.[17] Since they believe the attribution of the *Vaidalyaprakaraṇa* to Nāgārjuna "is based only in very weak grounds," they similary doubt the authenticity of the *Vigrahavyāvartanī*.[18] This is not the place to assess in detail their criticism of ascribing the *Vaidalyaprakaraṇa* to Nāgārjuna (although in themselves they do not strike me as any stronger than those presented against the *Vigrahavyāvartanī*). I am more concerned with the methodology of this argument. While one may agree with Tola and Dragonetti's claim that "an argument in favour of the authenticity based on the style and tenets of the work is not decisive by itself as any person belonging to the Mādhyamika school could have written in the style of the Master," the reverse of this procedure, making a claim *against* the authenticity of a text based on its similarity with another one faces its own problems.[19] For it cannot be a sufficient argument against the authenticity of a text A that it resembles a text B, which, for the time being, we assume to be not authentic. Otherwise we could use any Madhyamaka text B demonstrably not by Nāgārjuna to argue that a text A, such as the *Mūlamadhyamakakārikā* (usually taken to be a work of Nāgārjuna's by definition), was not in fact composed by Nāgārjuna, given that it resembles text B. What the critic would want to show is that the properties which make us doubt the authenticity of B are precisely the ones that make it resemble A. But if this is the case, the entire argument from resemblance is superfluous, for we could just use these properties of A to argue against its authenticity without bringing in B at all.

Apart from the fact that it is far from obvious that the *Vaidalyaprakaraṇa* ("text B") is not authentic Tola and Dragonetti do not seem to think that the

15. 1982a: 11.

16. Ruegg (1981: 21–23)

17. Lindtner (1982a: 87) agrees.

18. Tola and Dragonetti (1995: 15). In (1998: 155) they assert that the *Vaidalyaprakaraṇa* "cannot be attributed to Nāgārjuna," without, however, adducing any new evidence for this stronger claim.

19. For their arguments against the authenticity of the *Vaidalyaprakaraṇa*, see Tola and Dragonetti (1995: 7–15).

properties which should make us doubt the authenticity of the *Vaidalyaprakaraṇa* are the very same ones which should cast suspicion on the authorship of the *Vigrahavyāvartanī* ("text A").[20] For them, the main worry with the *Vaidalyaprakaraṇa* appears to be its "recourse to theories or opinions of the other schools", and "its numerous connections with so many texts, schools, and doctrines."[21] But this is not the case with the *Vigrahavyāvartanī*, nor do Tola and Dragonetti claim that it is in their 1998 paper. The main opponent of Nāgārjuna in this text, apart from the Ābhidharmika metaphysics which consitutes the background of all his philosophical discussion, is the Nyāya epistemology. And even though the Naiyāyikas are not mentioned in central works such as the *Mūlamadhyamakakārikā*, their presence is hardly a sufficient ground to question of authenticity of the *Vigrahavyāvartanī*.

This brings us to the second main point of criticism raised by Tola and Dragonetti against the *Vigrahavyāvartanī*. Their argument is based on the fact that there are *terms* which play a prominent role in the *Vigrahavyāvartanī* but are not found in the *Mūlamadhyamakakārikā* or other prominent members of the Yukti-corpus, such as the *Śūnyatāsaptati* and *Yuktiṣaṣṭikā*, and that *illustrative examples* found in these texts are used in a different way in the *Vigrahavyāvartanī*. The terms "epistemic instrument" (*pramāṇa*) and "epistemic object" (*prameya*) are not mentioned in the *Mūlamadhyamakakārikā*; in fact, there is very little epistemological discussion in this text at all. The example of the magically created persons mentioned in verse 23 of the *Vigrahavyāvartanī* is also found in the *Śūnyatāsaptati*, but there it is not used to argue for the causal efficiency of the agent. Tola and Dragonetti list numerous examples of this sort that are very interesting from a comparative perspective but do not present a strong case against the claim that the *Vigrahavyāvartanī* was composed by Nāgārjuna. For this argument to work, one would have to assume that an author generally discusses the same problems in all his works and that he generally uses examples in the same way. A brief look at any philosopher's literary output, past or present, will convince us how unrealistic his assumption is. Not only do philosophers treat different topics in different works but also their works sometimes disagree with each other (if this disagreement is diachronic, we generally regard it as philosophical development). In the present discussion, disagreements between the *Vigrahavyāvartanī* and Nāgārjuna's other main works are not even an issue. On the whole, the philosophical system presented is quite uniform. But if even the mere fact that different works deal with different aspects of the same theory are seen as sufficient to question the authenticity of some of them, one wonders what

20. Tola and Dragonetti (1995: 8). The majority of modern Madhyamaka scholars accept the *Vaidalyaprakaraṇa* as one of Nāgārjuna's works. See, for example, Kajiyama (1965: 130), Ruegg (1981: 19, 21), Lindtner (1982a: 11, 87).

21. Tola and Dragonetti (1995: 14).

would happen if we ever encounter the ancient Indian equivalent of the *Tractatus* and the *Philosophical Investigations*. Considering the diverging philosophical views discussed in each, we would surely have to assume that they were written by two different people who just happened to share the name Wittgenstein.

Structure of the *Vigrahavyāvartanī*

The structure of the *Vigrahavyāvartanī* is certainly peculiar. The objections are listed one after the other in the first part of the text, followed by all the replies in the second half. This makes it necessary to repeat nearly all of the first twenty verses in the second half in order to indicate which reply is aimed at which criticism. We do wonder why Nāgārjuna did not choose the far simpler method of simply listing one objection, followed by the reply, then another objection followed by its reply, and so on. It has been suggested that reason for this is that the first twenty verses were not in fact written by Nāgārjuna at all, so that the *Vigrahavyāvartanī* is really a conjunction of two texts by two different authors.[22]

But this does not appear to explain much, either. For if the *Vigrahavyāvartanī* was really written as the refutation of a specific treatise critical of Madhyamaka thought, it would have been more straightforward for Nāgārjuna to respond directly to this text and to quote the verses he sets out to refute at the respective parts of his discussion, very much as he does in the second part of the *Vigrahavyāvartanī*. By quoting just five more verses in this way, Nāgārjuna would have incorporated all of the root verses of the supposed anti-Madhyamaka treatise into his text, thereby making it superfluous to list them once more at the beginning of his treatise.

In addition, conceiving of the first twenty verses as an independent treatise raises about as many questions as it is supposed to answer. These verses do not set out a connected argument, but appear rather like a list of various criticisms one could raise against the Mādhyamikas. The perspectives from which these objections come are very diverse, so that it is difficult to see what the views of the supposed author of this treatise could possibly have been.

It is perhaps easier to understand the peculiarities of the *Vigrahavyāvartanī*'s arrangement by asking ourselves why Nāgārjuna saw it necessary to keep the majority of the objections together in one section of his text.[23] Perhaps a list

22. Tola and Dragonetti (1998: 154–155).

23. The opponent does speak occasionaly in the second half (for example in the autocommentary on verses 33, 37, 40, and 69). This may be seen as evidence for a certain autonomy of the first part, which would explain why not all of the objections have been included here. It would imply that Nāgārjuna drew a distinction between the objections somehow transmitted to him as belonging to one group, discussed in the first part, and other, merely hypothetical, objections he considered as part of his reply and included in the second part.

of disputed topics (the *vigraha* the title refers to) based on a variety of presuppositions (both Buddhist and non-Buddhist) had been circulating and tempted him to respond. If this list was well known enough for it to be recognizable but not detailed enough to serve as a basis for a treatise refuting it, the arrangement of the text might appear a bit more reasonable. By keeping the structure of the list intact, the aim and justification of his Madhyamaka countercritique would be evident; at the same time, the objections it contained had to be enlarged in order to present a satisfactory and determinate target. Nāgārjuna therefore formulated the list of objections as the first part of the *Vigrahavyāvartanī* in the same verse-plus-commentary form we find in the second part. This then made it necessary to quote a substantial amount of the verses from the first part in the second in order to match objections with replies.

The translation presented here follows the structure of the *Vigrahavyāvartanī*. For the commentary, however, I have chosen a different approach. The commentary incorporates the entire text of the *Vigrahavyāvartanī*.[24] It is, however, rearranged in such a way that the objections from the first part are followed directly by the respective replies from the second part. In this way verses 1 and 2, for example, are not followed by verse 3, but by verses 21 to 24, which answer the objection formulated there. In this way the *Vigrahavyāvartanī* is easier to follow as a philosophical text, since the opponent's objection and Nāgārjuna's reply illuminate one another. Moreover, this rearrangement allows us to divide the text into different sections of objections and replies that deal with different issues. It is thereby easier to see which groups of problems the *Vigrahavyāvartanī* deals with.

In the translation I have attempted to provide English equivalents of all the Indian philosophical terms and have only given the Sanskrit equivalent in brackets at times when I considered it to be indispensable. Translations of technical philosophical terms are, of course, always problematic, as it is usually not possible to find a precise conceptual equivalent in the target language. The most obvious example in the present text is the central term *svabhāva*, here translated as "substance." In an earlier discussion of Nāgārjuna's thought I left this term untranslated, arguing that none of the potential equivalents from Western philosophy cover all the dimensions of its meaning.[25] While I still believe this to be the case, the use of the term *svabhāva* in the *Vigrahavyāvartanī* shows a considerable amount of overlap with the term "substance," used to

24. Apart from the references to the objections from the first twenty verses ("Concerning what you said earlier [in verse *x*] we reply:") which are superfluous in the rearrangement. I also left out the formulaic phrases connecting some of the verses (*kiṃ cānyat*, "and, moreover, another issue"; *atra brūmaḥ* "on this point we reply," etc.)

25. Westerhoff (2009a: 4).

refer to an entity not depending on anything else.[26] Translating it in this way therefore keeps the translation free from unfamiliar technical terms and neologisms of "Buddhist Hybrid English" (such as "inherent existence," "own being"), while also giving a sufficiently accurate representation of Nāgārjuna's arguments.[27]

Synopsis of the Argument

In the commentary I divided the *Vigrahavyāvartanī* into ten sections.

1. *The Status of the Theory of Emptiness [1–4, 21–29]*

Nāgārjuna begins his treatise by presenting an objection that I have called the "Madhyamaka dilemma." Since the Madhyamaka sets out to defend the thesis of universal emptiness, which argues that all things without exception lack substance or *svabhāva*, the statement of the thesis will lack substance as well. But this leads to a problem, the opponent says. For how could a wholly insubstantial thesis be effective as an argument against any philosophical proposition? But if it is not effective in this way, it also cannot refute the substantialist's view that substances do exist and is therefore argumentationally powerless. This is the first horn of the dilemma. On the other hand, if it *does* have argumentative power it must be substantial, so that the universal thesis that *everything* lacks substance has to be false. This is the second horn.

Nāgārjuna responds to this problem by embracing the first horn. Since the thesis of universal emptiness is causally produced, it is itself empty. The thesis therefore holds with full generality. As the examples used by the opponent show, he has misunderstood "empty" to mean "non-existent," which explains why he questions the ability of empty objects to accomplish anything. But Nāgārjuna states explicitly that empty objects are causally efficacious. In fact, as being empty means being arisen in dependence on causes and conditions, this emptiness is a precondition for objects' being able to enter into a causal nexus in turn. To this extent, the first horn of the dilemma is not an unacceptable consequence but an essential part of the theory of emptiness.

The causal efficacy of empty objects is illustraded by Nāgārjuna using several examples. The most mundane ones are those of things like chariots, pots, and so forth, which are dependently originated (and therefore empty) while

26. 'Substance' is unfortunately also commonly used to translate the term *dravya*. For an overview of the different conceptual dimensions of the notion of *svabhāva* in Nāgārjuna's thought, see Westerhoff (2009a: chapter 2).

27. Westerhoff (2009a: Introduction, chapter 2).

at the same time obviously capable of fulfilling a variety of functions. More intriguingly, he describes several cases where causal interaction happens between illusory entities, such as various phantoms conjured up by an illusionist. Nobody will want to hold that these phantoms exist substantially, yet they interact in a regular, causal manner.

This section also contains the famous twenty-ninth verse in which Nāgārjuna claims that he does not have any thesis himself. This does not amount to the paradoxical claim of someone asserting that he is not asserting anything. What Nāgārjuna wants to say is that he does not hold any substantially existent thesis, that is, any thesis which is to be supplied with a realist semantics that spells out meaning and truth in terms of correspondence with a mind-independent reality. The Mādhyamika will have to interpret his statements in terms of a purely convention-based semantics in order to avoid reintroducing substantially existent objects by the back door.

2. *Epistemology [5–6, 30–51]*

This is by far the longest of all sections in the *Vigrahavyāvartanī*. Considering only the amount of text it occupies, one might think that it took Nāgārjuna twenty-one verses in order to reply to an objection described in two. This, however, is not the case.

The opponent is still worried about how empty things can be functionally efficient, and argues that the four instruments of epistemic access to the world traditionally accepted—perception, inference, testimony, and likeness—cannot provide any basis for our knowledge of the world if they, like everything else, are regarded as empty.

Nāgārjuna does not spend the remainder of the section replying to this by repeating his claim for the equivalence of emptiness and functionality just made. Instead, he presents a comprehensive critique of the epistemology his Nyāya opponent defends. First, Nāgārjuna points out that if we try to justify our knowledge of the world by saying that we acquired it by accepted epistemic instruments, we have just pushed the problem back one step, for we now have to justify the instruments.

Two replies suggest themselves here: first, we could say that each epistemic instrument is established by another, distinct epistemic instrument, or that they do not need any establishement at all. In the first case we are faced with an infinite regress, since each instrument requires a new instrument to establish it. That we need infintely many epistemic instruments in this way is not the greatest problem here (one might want to hold that the epistemic instruments establish each other in a circular fashion, so that only finitely many of them would be required), but rather the fact that we never reach any foundation for our epistemological theory, that is, something which tells us *why* what we regard to be epistemic instruments really are such instruments.

The second reply, arguing that the epistemic instruments do not need to be established in turn, is not very attractive because the Naiyāyika wants to claim that *all* we know is known by some epistemic instrument. But knowing that the epistemic instruments really are the instruments they seem to be then would be something that we could not know by these very instruments.

The opponent suggests an alternative that is supposed to get around these problems. In the same way in which fire illuminates both other things as well as itself, he argues, the epistemic instruments can establish both: the things to be known as well as themselves. Nāgārjuna uses the next six verses (34–39) in order to defuse the force of this example by arguing that fire does not in fact illuminate itself. Should the opponent still hold on to the thesis of the self-establishment of the epistemic instruments despite the unsatisfactory fire example, Nāgārjuna continues in verse 40, there is yet another problem in store. For how do we know that the self-establishment of the epistemic instruments really is an indication of epistemic veracity and not of something else? We can only do so by looking at the objects thus apprehended. But if we have to take the epistemic objects into account, the claim of self-establishment loses its basis.

The next seven verses (42–48) take a closer look at the role of the objects in the establishment of the epistemic instruments. Establishing the epistemic instruments on the basis of the objects does not seem to be a very promising route. After all, the instruments are supposed to be what provides us with knowledge of the objects. The objects cannot really be taken to be independent of the epistemic instruments, either, since then there would be no point in having the instruments to establish the objects in the first place. Finally, if the epistemic instruments and objects are mutually dependent on each other, we do not reach a foundation for our epistemology.

Nāgārjuna therefore concludes that the we have to give up the idea that epistemic instruments and objects are epistemic instruments and objects intrinsically, that is that there is a collection of objects "out there," the existence of which is independent of our epistemic endeavors, and a set of epistemic detectors "in here" that exist independent of the objects they detect. It therefore becomes evident that it is in no way a drawback that we have to regard the epistemic instruments as empty, as the opponent suggested at the beginning of this section. Given the problems of the alternative picture he provides, this is in fact the preferable option.

3. Intrinsically Good Things [7–8, 52–56]

In the preceding section, the opponent argued from the perspective of Nyāya epistemology. Now we see him take the standpoint of a Buddhist, probably that of an Ābhidharmika. The opponent suggests that the Buddha's teaching implies that at least some things must exist substantially, namely, those which are regarded as fundamentally bad (such as suffering) and those which are regarded as fundamentally good (such as liberation). These are not just bad or good because we think them to be that way, but they have these qualities by their very nature, and exist independent of anything else. By denying the substantial existence of these properties, Nāgārjuna invalidates core assumptions of the Buddhist doctrine.

Nāgārjuna replies by pointing out that in fact matters are the other way around. It is the opponent who cannot make sense of the Buddhist path. For if suffering and liberation existed as substances, independent of other things, it would be impossible ever to eradicate suffering or bring about liberation, since they would be outside of the network of causes and conditions. This is another manifestation of the claim that the theory of emptiness does not contradict causal efficiency but is rather one of its essential preconditions.

4. Names without Objects [9, 57–59]

The critcism raised here has to be understood against the background of a Nyāya-style realist semantics. According to this theory, simple names and predicates of a language acquire their meaning by connecting with things and properties in the world. But then, if Nāgārjuna denies the existence of substance, he is faced with the problem that the term "substance" only gets its meaning by picking out a corresponding thing in the world. In this case his assertion must be wrong, as we can argue on semantic grounds that substance must exist.

It is indeed not very surprising that we run into problems if we couple a semantic theory like the one defended by the Naiyāyika, which postulates a foundation of language in the world, with an anti-foundationalist position like Nāgārjuna's theory of emptiness. But there is no reason why Nāgārjuna should have to adopt the Nyāya theory of language. Taking into account the realist assumptions built into this semantics, he would be ill-advised to do so. But if this semantics is rejected, the criticism raised will disappear.

5. Extrinsic Substances [10, 60]

But perhaps there is a way of squaring a realist semantics with the theory of emptiness. We could assume that substance does exist, so that the term "substance" is guaranteed to have a referent, but that this substance does not exist anywhere in the world, so that Nāgārjuna's theory of universal emptiness comes out as true.

This suggestion made by the opponent faces a number of difficulties, the least of which seems to be that our language will persistently refer to things other than those we think it refers to. We might think that in referring to a thing we refer to the thing's substance, but in fact we are refering to a substance existing somehow apart from the thing. Fortunately, Nāgārjuna does not have to solve this problem, since for him there is no particular reason to save the realist's semantic theory. Since he does not presuppose the Naiyāyika's theory of language, there is no necessity for him to make it consistent with his theory of emptiness.

6. Negation and Existence [11–12, 61–64]

Once more this criticism only makes sense against the background of the Nyāya theory of language. Since all the simple terms in a statement have to connect with entities in the world, a statement like "the book is not on the table" can only be a statement of a local absence.[28] It can say that the book is not on the table only if the book exists somewhere else (for example, on the shelf), since otherwise the term "book" would not be able to refer. Interpreted in this way, Nāgārjuna's statement that there is no substance would similarly only be able to say a certain thing lacks substance, but not that substance does not exist altogether. So once again it seems that if Nāgārjuna's statement is meaningful it must be false.

Unfortunately for the opponent, this argument can also be run the other way around. If the statement "emptiness does not exist" is meaningful, "emptiness" must have a referent and thereby exist, which the opponent denies. The statement is therefore false. If it is true, however, it must be meaningless, since one of its terms is lacking a referent.

The way out of this difficulty, where each side accuses the other of asserting something either false or meaningless, is to give up the attempt of reconciling Nāgārjuna's theory of emptiness with the Nyāya semantics. One we reject this semantic doctrine, the problem disappears.

The opponent now worries whether Nāgārjuna's assertion of universal emptiness might, if feasible, not simply be pointless. We only assert negations of things we sometimes experience as conjoined, such as books and tables. But according to Nāgārjuna, we could not possibly observe any substances in the

28. Assuming for the sake of argument that all the terms in the statement are simple.

world, since there are no substances. Asserting such a negation therefore does not serve any practical purpose.

If it is not necessary to use language to negate non-existent objects the fact that Nāgārjuna finds it necessary to employ language to establish his negation means that he cannot be talking about a non-existent object. But if the substance he negates is existent, the process of negation must somehow make an existent thing nonexistent, which appears problematic. Nāgārjuna denies that negation has to accomplish this, and argues that his negation only makes the non-existence of substance known but does not bring it about. The point of his negation is not to make something existent nonexistent, but to remove a mistaken superimposition of substance onto the world.

7. The Mirage Analogy [13–13, 65–67]

The opponent suggests a way in which Nāgārjuna's negation of substance could be understood, by means of an example that is mentioned frequently in the Buddhist literature. This is the example of illusory water being perceived in a mirage. Even though there is no water in the mirage, the assertion of the statement "there is no water in the mirage" still has a point if directed at people who do not realize that the mirage is a mirage. But if he wants to use this example, then Nāgārjuna has to accept that the perception of the mirage exists, as well as whatever it is that caused the mirage, together with the perceiver of the mirage. Similarly, the negation of the appearance, what the negation negates, and the negator will also have to exist. In the same way in which it cannot be the case that all of these are as illusory as the water in the mirage, the opponent argues, Nāgārjuna's argument for emptiness only works if there are some things that are not empty.

Nāgārjuna considers the mirage analogy to be a useful illustration of the theory of emptiness. However, it can be spelled out in a way that avoids the difficulties just mentioned.

The perception of water in the mirage cannot be regarded as substantial, as something that exists dependent only on itself, but not on other things. It is a phenomenon that only arises based on external and some perceptual factors, and would not otherwise exist. As such, it is a very good example of an empty object. It is only because the illusory water exists in such a dependent manner that we can see through the appearance and ascertain the mirage as in fact waterless (instead of filled with invisible water). Since the other entities mentioned by the opponent can similarly argued to be empty, Nāgārjuna concludes that neither the illusory mirage nor empty objects in the world require nonempty, substantial foundations.

8. Emptiness and Reasons [17–19, 68]

This objection is a variation on a now-familiar theme. Nāgārjuna has to provide a reason for his thesis of universal emptiness. But to be consistent with the thesis, the reason has to be empty too. Given the opponent's reservations concerning the efficacy of empty objects, how can the reason be efficacious in a proof? Nāgārjuna cannot just argue that his thesis can be established without a reason, for in this case the opponent could claim the same about his denial of Nāgārjuna's thesis. But if there has to be a (non-empty) reason, Nāgārjuna's thesis cannot be correct.

Given that this point has been addressed several times before, Nāgārjuna's response is very brief. In particular, he points out that this difficulty can be resolved by appeal to the example of the mirage discussed previously. The statement "there is no water in the mirage" is, like all statements, empty of substance. Yet it fulfils a causal role by keeping the deluded travelers from rushing toward the illusory water. There is no conflict between the causal efficacy and the emptiness of a phenomenon.

9. Negation and Temporal Relations [20, 69]

This section discusses a worry about the temporal relation between a negation and the object it negates. The worry is a general one, but it acquires its special relevance in the present case because Nāgārjuna's thesis of universal emptiness is a negative claim.

We usually assume that during the process of thinking we construct some mental contents first and subsequently apply various cognitive operations (such as negation, conjunction, disjunction, and so forth) to these. If there is a causal process involved here, this is in fact the only way of conceiving of the application of cognitive operations. As causes temporally precede their effects, negation and negated object cannot be simultaneous, nor can the negation of the negated object exist before that very object.

But in this case there is a problem for the Naiyāyika. In the same way in which for him simple terms are guaranteed to refer, simple perceptions can never be erroneous. Error arises at the level of judgment, when correct simple perceptions are put together in the wrong way. However, once we have a correct perception, negating it can only lead to falsity, otherwise it would not have been correct in the first place.

Even though Nāgārjuna endorses the general criticism of the temporal relation between cause and effect of which this special problem is a particular instance, he does not agree that it rules out negations like the theory of universal emptiness. This is because he does not agree that the object of negation is something apprehended by a correct perception; he rather thinks of it along the lines of the illusory water in the mirage. In this case the illusion exists first, and its negation later, and there is no difficulty in understanding how the negation accomplishes the refutation of the illusion.

The opponent finally tries to backtrack by arguing that perhaps it is possible that cause and effect are related by temporal relations in the familiar way. Nāgārjuna refers to the usual Madhyamaka arguments against this and concludes by remarking that, if the opponent really thought these temporal relations were possible, the entire criticism in this section would have been without a point.

10. Conclusion [70]

The final section of the *Vigrahavyāvartanī* stresses once more one of Nāgārjuna's central claims, namely, that his theory of universal emptiness does not conflict with the conventional truth that objects stand in causal relations and can fulfil specific functions. On the contrary, Nāgārjuna argues that his theory is a precondition of this conventional truth. As such, emptiness provides the basis both for everyday worldly existence as well as for the path leading beyond it.

2

Text

The Dispeller of Disputes

Veneration to the Buddha!

1. **If the substance of all things is not to be found anywhere, your assertion which is devoid of substance is not able to refute substance.**

If the substance of things was not found anywhere, in the causes, in the conditions, or in the combination of the causes and the conditions, and if it is also not separate from these, it is said: "all things are empty".

For the sprout does not exist in the seed which is its cause; it does not exist in each one of earth, water, fire, wind, and so forth, which are agreed to be its conditions; it does not exist in the combinations of conditions; not in the combinations of causes and conditions; not in the combination of causes and conditions, nor does it exist as separate from these, free from causes and conditions.

As substance does not exist anywhere here, the sprout is without substance, and since it is without substance it is empty. As this sprout without substance is empty because of its lack of substance, in the same way all things are empty as well because of their lack of substance.

Here we say: If it is like this, your assertion, which claims that "all things are empty," is also empty. Why? Because your assertion does not exist in the cause: it does not exist in the great elements collectively or individually.

It does also not exist in the conditions which are the action of the chest, the throat, the lips, the tongue, the root of the teeth, the palate, the nose, the head and so forth; it does not exist in the combination of the causes and the conditions; and it also does not exist as separate from this, free from the combination of causes and conditions. Since it does not exist anywhere among these, it is without substance. Since it is without substance, it is empty. For this reason it is impossible that it dispels the substance of all things. Why?

This is because a non-existent fire cannot burn, a non-existent knife cannot cut, a non-existent water cannot moisten. In the same way, a non-existent assertion cannot negate the substance of all things. Therefore your statement that the substance of all things has been negated everywhere, that the substance of things has been dispelled everywhere, is not tenable.

2. Moreover, if that statement exists substantially, your earlier thesis is refuted. There is an inequality to be explained, and the specific reason for this should be given.

Moreover, you could think that there should not be this mistake by arguing, "This statement exists substantially and because it is a substance it is not empty. Therefore it negates the substance of all things, dispells the substance of all things." We say in reply: If it is like this, your earlier thesis that all things are empty is refuted.

Furthermore, your statement is also included in all things. How can it be that while all things are empty your assertion by which, because of its non-emptiness, the substance of all things is negated is not empty? Thus a controversy involving six points ensues. How again is this?

1. Look, if all things are empty, this implies that your statement is empty too because it is included among all things. Because of that emptiness, the negation fails to be accomplished. Therefore the negation "all things are empty" fails to be accomplished.
2. If, however, the negation "all things are empty" is accomplished, this implies that your assertion is also not empty. Because of the non-emptiness, the negation fails to be accomplished by this.
3. But if all things are empty and your assertion, by which the negation is achieved, is not empty, this implies that your assertion is not included among all things. There is a contradiction by the example.
4. If, however, your assertion is included among all things, if all things are empty, this implies that your assertion is also empty. And because it is empty it cannot accomplish a negation.
5. Then, assume your assertion was empty and by it the negation "everything is empty" was established. But in that case all empty things would be causally efficacious, and this is not admissible.

6. Assume then that all things are empty and lack causal efficacy, and let there be no contradiction by the example. Having assumed this, however, your empty assertion fails to accomplish the negation of the substance of all things.

Furthermore, because your statement exists, there is an inequality as a consequence: some things are empty, some things are not empty. And while there is such an inequality, it is necessary to give the specific reason by which something would be empty or not empty. That, however, has not been specified. In this context, your statement "all things are empty" is not tenable. Moreover:

3. If you were of the opinion that it is like "do not make a sound," this would not be adequate, for in this case there is the prevention of a future sound by an existing one.

You might be of the opinion that certainly someone who said "you should not make a sound" would himself make a sound, and that by this sound there would be the prevention of that other one's sound. In precisely this way the empty statement "all things are empty" dispels the substance of all things.

Here we say: This is also fails to be accomplished. Why? For in this case the negation of a future sound is brought about by an existent sound. However, for you here the negation of the substance of all things is not brought about by an existent assertion. For according to your opinion, the assertion is non-existent and the substance of all things is also non-existent. To this extent, saying that your statement is like "do not make a sound" is an unsuitable assertion. Furthermore:

4. If you thought that the negation's negation is also like this, that would indeed not be correct. Thus your thesis, not mine, is corrupted by the specific characteristic.

You might think "By this very rule the negation's negation fails to be accomplished, and in this context your negating the assertion of the negation of the substance of all things fails to be accomplished."

Here we say: This is also not correct. Why? Since the specific characteristic of the thesis applies to your thesis, not to mine. In this context you say "all things are empty," I do not. The initial position is not mine. In this context, your statement that while it is like this, the negation's negation fails to be accomplished is not tenable. Moreover:

5. If you deny objects after having apprehended them through perception, that perception by which the objects are perceived does not exist.

If, having apprehended all things by perception, one then negates the things by saying "all things are empty," that fails to be accomplished. Why? Because it is included among all things, perception, the epistemic instrument, is also empty. Who conceives of objects is empty as well. To this extent there is no thing apprehended by perception, the epistemic instrument. The negation of something unperceived fails to be established. In that context, the statement "all things are empty" fails to be accomplished.

You might think, "The rejection of all things is brought about after having apprehended them either by inference, testimony, or likeness." Here we say:

6. Inference, testimony, and likeness are refuted by perception, as well as the objects to be established by inference, testimony, and example.

Inference, testimony, and likeness are refuted by perception, the epistemic instrument. For as perception, the epistemic instrument, is empty because of the emptiness of all things, in the same way inference, likeness, and testimony are also empty because of the emptiness of all things. The objects to be established by inference and the objects to be established by testimony and likeness are also empty because of the emptiness of all things. Who apprehends things by inference, likeness, and testimony is also empty. Therefore there is no apprehending of things, and for things which are not apprehended the negation of substance fails to be established. In that context, the statement "all things are empty" is not tenable. Moreover:

7. People who know the state of things think that auspicious phenomena have an auspicious substance. This distinction also holds for the other things.

In this context, people who know the state of things have the 119 auspicious things in mind.

Thus the following are auspicious in one of their aspects: (1) cognition, (2) feeling, (3) discrimination, (4) volition, (5) touch, (6) attention, (7) aspiration, (8) devotion, (9) effort, (10) memory, (11) meditative stabilization, (12) wisdom, (13) equanimity, (14) practice, (15) complete practice, (16) attainment, (17) noble intention, (18) freedom from anger, (19) joy, (20) effort, (21) zeal, (22) connection with ignorance, (23) perseverance, (24) freedom from obstacles, (25) possession of power, (26) aversion, (27) absence of repentance, (28) grasping, (29) not grasping, (30) recollection, 31) firmness, (32) special adherence, (33) freedom from effort, (34) freedom from delusion, (35) freedom from exertion, (36) striving, (37) aspiration, (38) satisfaction, (39) being disjoint from the object, (40) being not conducive to liberation, (41) birth, (42) enduring, (43) impermanence, (44) possession, (45) old age, (46) utter torment, (47) dissatisfaction, (48) deliberation, (49) pleasure, (50) clarity, (51) grasping the discordant, (52) affection, (53) discordance, (54) grasping the concordant, (55) fearlessness, (56) reverence, (57) veneration, (58) devotion, (59) lack of devotion, (60) obedience, (61) respect, (62) lack of respect, (63) suppleness, (64) ebullience, (65) speech, (66) agitation, (67) attainment, (68) lack of faith, (69) lack of suppleness, (70) purification, (71) steadfastness, (72) gentleness, (73) repentance, (74) anguish,

(75) confusion, (76) arrogance, (77) grasping the unfavorable, (78) doubt, (79) pure discipline, (80) inner serenity, (81) fear; moreover, there is (82) faith, (83) bashfulness, (84) rectitude, (85) being not deceived, (86) pacification, (87) being without fickleness, (88) conscientiousness, (89) kindness, (90) discriminating comprehension, (91) freedom from anger, (92) freedom from desire, (93) lack of self-infatuation, (94) lack of attachment, (95) lack of hatred, (96) lack of ignorance, (97) omniscience, (98) non-abandonment, (99) affluence, (100) modesty, (101) lack of concealment, (102) unobstructed intention, (103) compassion, (104) loving kindness, (105) non-discouragement, (106) absence of passion, (107) magical powers, (108) lack of attachment, (109) lack of envy, (110) a mind free from eradication, (111) patience, (112) renunciation, (113) lack of gentleness, (114) being in accordance with one's resources, (115) merit, (116) attainment of the state of non-conception, (117) being conducive to liberation, (118) lack of omniscience, (119) uncompounded phenomena.

In this way the 119 auspicious things have an auspicious substance. In the same way, the inauspicious things have an inauspicious substance; the obscured-neutral mental states are substantially obscured-neutral mental states; the non-obscured-neutral mental states are substantially non-obscured-neutral mental states; what is called desire has a substance that is called desire; what is called matter has a substance that is called matter; what is called immaterial has a substance that is called immaterial; uncontaminated things have an uncontaminated substance; what is called suffering, its origin, its cessation, and the path leading to cessation has a substance that is called suffering, its cessation, and the path leading to its cessation; that which is to be abandoned by meditation has a substance which is to be abandoned by meditation; that which is not to be abandoned has a substance that is not to be abandoned.

As far as different kinds of substances of things are evident in this way, the statement made in this context "all things are insubstantial, and because of insubstantiality they are empty" is not tenable. Moreover:

8. The phenomena of liberation have the substance of phenomena of liberation. The same holds for those things which have been mentioned in connection with the state of things, as well as for those things which are not phenomena of liberation.

Here things which have been mentioned in connection with the state of things, as well as those conducive to liberation, have a substance conducive to liberation. Those which are not conducive to liberation have a substance not conducive to liberation, the limbs of enlightenment have a substance which is the limbs of enlightenment, those which are not the limbs of enlightenment have a substance which is not the limbs of enlightenment, the factors harmonious with enlightenment have a substance which is harmonious with enlightenment, those which are not harmonious with enlightenment have a substance which is not harmonious with enlightenment. The same holds for the remaining ones.

So far as different kinds of substances of things are evident in this way, because of this the statement "all things are insubstantial, and because of insubstantiality they are empty" is not tenable. Moreover:

9. And if there was no substance, there would also not even be the name "insubstantiality of things," for there is no name without a referent.

And if the substance of all things were not to exist, there would be the absence of substance. There would also not be the name "absence of substance". Why? For there is no name whatsoever without a referent. Therefore, because the name exists, there is the substance of things, and because substance exists all things are non-empty. Therefore the statement "all things are without substance, because of being without substance they are empty" is not tenable. Moreover:

10. Rather, substance exists, yet the substance of things does not exist. It has to be explained to what this thingless substance belongs.

You might rather think: "Let there not be a name without referent. Substance is produced, but the substance of things is not brought about in turn. In this way the emptiness of things will be established because of the absence of substance of things. And there is no name without referent."

Here we say: The object to which the thingless substance of the object belongs needs to be explained. But this is not explained. So far the assumption "substance exists but this in turn is not the substance of things" is deficient. Moreover:

11. To the extent to which the negation "there is no pot in the house" is precisely a negation of an existent, your negation is a negation of an existing substance.

In this case the negation of an existent object, not of a non-existent one, is brought about. Thus the statement "there is no pot in the house" brings about the negation of an existent, not of a non-existent pot. Just in this way, the statement "there is no substance of things" achieves the negation of an existent substance, not of a non-existent one. In this context, the statement "all things are insubstantial, and because of insubstantiality they are empty" is not tenable. Precisely because the negation is brought about, the substance of all things is not refuted.

12. Now as this substance does not exist, what is negated by that statement of yours? For the negation of a non-existent is accomplished without words.

As this substance does indeed not exist, what do you negate by that statement "all things are insubstantial"? For the negation of a non-existent is established without words; it is like that for the coolness of fire or the solidity of water. Moreover:

13. As ignorant people wrongly perceive water in a mirage, in the same way there would be a wrong perception for you in this case, for a non-existent object is negated.

You might think: "Ignorant people wrongly perceive water in a mirage, and the learned ones say 'surely this mirage is waterless' in order to dispel this perception. In the same way, the statement 'all things are insubstantial' is made in order to dispel the beings' perception of substance in things without substance." Here we say:

14. Yet, while it exists in this way, there are these six things: the perception, the perceived, and the perceiver of that object; the negation, the object of negation, and the negator.

If it is thus, there is indeed the perception by beings, there is the perceived, and there are those beings who perceive that object. There is also the negation of what is wrongly perceived, there is the object of negation, which is just the wrongly perceived object, and the negators of that perception, people like you; these six things are established. Because these six things are established, the statement "all things are empty" is not tenable.

15. But if there is just no perception, no perceived, and no perceiver, then there is certainly no negation, no object of negation, and no negator.

But by making the statement "there should not be that fault," while there just is no perception, no perceived, and no perceiver according to this, the negation of the perception, namely, "all things are insubstantial," does also not exist; there is also no object of negation, there is also no negator.

16. While there is neither negation, object of negation, nor negator, all things are established, and so is their substance.

While there is no negation, no object of negation, and no negator, all things are unnegated and the substance of all things exists. Moreover:

17. Your reason is not established. Because there is no substance, where then does your reason come from? Moreover, no matter is established without a reason.

The reason for your statement "all things are without substance" is not established. Why? Because of the lack of substance, all things are empty. Therefore, where does the reason come from? While there is no reason, where does the establishment of the statement "all things are empty," which is without reason, come from? In this context, the statement "all things are empty" is not tenable. Moreover:

18. And if the denial of substance is established for you without a reason, the existence of substantiality is also established for me without a reason.

If you thought: "The insubstantiality of things is established without reason," then as far as the denial of substance is established for you without a reason, so far the existence of substance is also established for me without a reason.

19. If the reason exists, the "absence of substance of things" fails to be accomplished. For nowhere in the world is there anything without substance.

In this context, if you thought that the reason exists, the "insubstantiality of all things" fails to be accomplished. Why? For in the world there is no thing which is without substance.

20. Supposing that the negation is earlier, and the negated later fails to be successful. And being later and being simultaneous fail to be successful. Therefore substance exists.

In this context, supposing that the negation is earlier and the negated, what is lacking substance, later is not successful. For while there is no object of negation, what is the negation a negation of?

Moreover, supposing that the negation is later and the object of negation earlier is also not successful. For once the object of negation is established, what does the negation do?

If we suppose that the negation and the object of negation are simultaneous, then the negation is not the cause of the object to be negated and the object of negation is not the cause of the negation. In the same way, considering the two horns of a cow, which have arisen simultaneously, it is clearly not the case that the right one is the cause of the left or the left the cause of the right.

In this context, the statement "all things are without substance" is not tenable.

In this context, regarding what you said, "**1. If the substance of all things is not to be found anywhere, your assertion which is devoid of substance is not able to refute substance,**" we reply:

21. If my speech is not in the combination of causes and conditions and also not distinct from them, is it not the case that emptiness is established because of the absence of the substance of things?

If my speech is not in the cause, not among the great elements, neither in the collection of conditions nor distinct from it, if it is not in the action of the chest, the throat, the lips, the root of the teeth, the palate, the nose, the head, and so forth, if it is not in the combination of those, is not free from the combination of causes and conditions, not distinct from them—to this extent it is without substance, and because it is without substance it is empty. Thus is it not the case that the emptiness of my speech is established because of its lack of substance? And as the speech of mine is empty because of the lack of substance, so all things are also empty because of the lack of substance. In this context, your statement "the emptiness of all things is not established because of the emptiness of your speech" is not tenable. Moreover:

22. The dependent existence of things is said to be emptiness, for what is dependently existent is lacking substance.

You do not understand the meaning of the emptiness of things. Not knowing the meaning of emptiness, you formulate the following criticism: "The negation of the substance of things is not established because of the emptiness of your speech." In this context, the dependent existence of things is emptiness. Why? Because of insubstantiality. Those things which are dependently arisen are not endowed with substance, because there is no substance. Why? Because of the dependence on causes and conditions. If things existed substantially they would exist without causes and conditions; however, they do not exist in this way. Therefore they are said to be without substance, and because they are without substance, empty. Therefore it follows that in the same way my own speech is without substance, because it is dependently arisen, and because it is without substance it is empty.

For instance a chariot, pot, cloth, and so forth, which are empty of substance because they are dependently originated, perform in their respective ways by removing wood, grass, earth, by containing honey, water, or milk, and by bringing forth protection against cold, wind, or heat. Similarly my speech, which is also without substance because it is dependently arisen, plays a part in establishing the lack of substance of things. In this context, the statement "Because of the absence of substance there is the emptiness of your statement, and because of the emptiness of that statement it fails to accomplish the negation of the substance of all things" is not tenable. Moreover:

23. Suppose one artificial being were to hinder another artificial being, or an illusory man would hinder one brought about by his own illusionistic power. This negation would be just like that.

It would be as if an artificial man hindered another artificial man engaged in some action or as if an illusory man brought forth by an illusionist would hinder another illusory man engaged in some action who was brought forth by the illusory man's own illusory power. In this case the artificial man who is hindered is empty, as is the one who hinders him. The illusory man who is hindered is empty, as is the one who hinders him. Therefore in just the same way the negation of the substance of all things is established by my empty speech. In this context, your statement "The negation of the substance of all things is not established by your speech because of its emptiness" is not tenable. The discussion in six points mentioned by you is also refuted by this. Indeed, while it is like that my speech does not fail to be included among all things. There is nothing non-empty, also it is not the case that all things are non-empty.

Concerning what you said earlier, "**2. Moreover, if that statement exists substantially, your earlier thesis is refuted. There is an inequality to be explained, and the reason for this should be given,**" we reply:

24. This speech does not exist substantially, therefore there is no destruction of my position. There is no inequality, and no particular reason to be mentioned.

So far, since my speech is dependently originated it is not established substantially. As was said before, because it is not substantially established it is empty. As far as my speech is empty and all the other things are also empty, there is no inequality. If we say "this speech is not empty, yet all the other things are empty," there would be an inequality. But it is not like this and therefore there is no inequality.

And as far as the inequality of us saying "that speech is not empty; however, all the other things are empty" does not arise, to that extent we do not have to give the special reason as in, "by this reason that speech is not empty, however, all things are empty."

In this context, your statement "there is the destruction of your thesis, there is an inequality, and you should state the special reason" is not tenable. Concerning what you said earlier, "**3. If you were of the opinion that your statement is like 'do not make a sound,' this would not be adequate, for in this case there is the prevention of a future sound by an existing one,**" we reply:

25. You did not construct the example "do not make a sound" successfully. That is the prevention of a sound by a sound, but it is clearly not like this in the present case.

This is not our example. In case someone said "do not make a sound," words are uttered and by them further utterances are prevented. Yet our empty statement does not prevent emptiness in a similar way. Why? There, in the example, sound is dispelled by sound. But it is not like this in the present case. We say "all objects are without substance, and because they are without substance they are empty." Why?

26. If substanceless things are refuted by something substanceless, when what is substanceless is abandoned substance would be established.

When an utterance prevents further utterances, as in the example of "do not make a sound," the example would be appropriate if a substanceless utterance prevented substanceless things. However, in this case the negation of the substance in things is brought about by substanceless speech. In this way, if the negation of the lack of substance in things was brought about by a substanceless speech, things would be endowed with substance because of this very negation of substancelessness. Because of being endowed with substance, they would not be empty. We declared the emptiness of things, not their non-emptiness. The example mentioned is a non-example.

27. The case is rather like an artificial person preventing someone's wrong notion, when that one thinks "this is a woman" about an artificial woman.

If some man had a wrong conception of an artificial woman empty of substance, thinking "this is really a woman," he might develop desire for her because of that wrong notion. The Blessed One or one of his disciples could then create an artificial man, and by the power of the Blessed One or of his disciple the man's wrong grasping would be prevented. In exactly the same way, the grasping at substance, which is like the artificial woman, is prevented and negated by my empty speech, which is like the artificial man. So this is a suitable example for establishing emptiness, not the one just given.

28. It is rather that the example is of the same nature as what we want to establish, for there is no existence of sound. We do not speak without assenting to the conventional truth.

The example "do not make a sound" is precisely of the same nature as what we want to establish. Why? Because things are uniformly without substance. There is no substantial existence of that sound because it is dependently arisen. Because there is no substantial existence of it your statement "**3.** [...] **for in this case there is the prevention of a future sound by an existing one**" is refuted.

Moreover, we do not speak without assenting to the conventional truth, rejecting the conventional truth when we say "all things are empty." For it is not without having had recourse to the conventional truth that the nature of things can be explained. As it was said:

> Not having had recourse to the conventional, the absolute is not taught. Without having approached the absolute, liberation is not reached.

To this extent all things are empty like my speech, and insubstantiality is established in both ways. Concerning what you said earlier, "**4. If you thought that the negation's negation is also like this, that would indeed not be correct. Thus your thesis, not mine, is corrupted by the specific characteristic,**" we reply:

29. If I had any thesis, that fault would apply to me. But I do not have any thesis, so there is indeed no fault for me.

If I had any thesis, the earlier fault you mentioned would apply to me, because the mark of my thesis has been affected. But I do not have any thesis. To that extent, while all things are empty, completely pacified, and by nature free from substance, from where could a thesis come? From where could something affecting the character of my thesis come? In this context your statement "there is precisely that fault for you, because the mark of your thesis has been affected" is not tenable.

Concerning what you said earlier, "**5. If you deny objects after having apprehended them through perception that perception by which the objects are perceived does not exist**" and "**6. Inference, testimony, and likeness are refuted by perception, as well as the objects to be established by inference, testimony, and example,**" we reply:

30. If I perceived anything by means of perception, I would affirm or deny. But because that does not exist, there is no criticism applicable to me.

If I apprehended any object by the causes of knowledge, by perception, inference, likeness, or authority, or by any particular one of the four epistemic instruments, I would indeed affirm or deny. But because I do not propound any object I do not affirm or deny.

In this context, your criticism is this: "If you deny any objects after having apprehended them by one of the epistemic instruments, such as perception and so forth, while these epistemic instruments do not exist, there are also no objects accessed by these epistemic instruments." But this criticism does not apply to me.

31. If according to you objects of some kind are established by the epistemic instruments, you have to indicate how according to you the epistemic instruments are established in turn.

If you think that epistemic objects of some kind are established through the epistemic instruments, just as a measuring instrument establishes what is to be measured, then where does the establishment of the four epistemic instruments, perception, inference, likeness, and testimony, come from? Because if the epistemic instruments were established by something that was not an epistemic instrument, the thesis that "the objects are established through the epistemic instruments" is refuted. Moreover:

32a. If the epistemic instruments were established by other epistemic instruments, there would be an infinite regress.

If you thought that the epistemic objects are established by the epistemic instruments, and that the epistemic instruments are established by other epistemic instruments, the absurd consequence of an infinite regress follows. What is the problem with the absurd consequence of an infinite regress?

32b. Neither the beginning, the middle, nor the end is established there.

There is the absurd consequence of an infinite regress, the beginning is not established. Why? Because those epistemic instruments are established by other epistemic instruments, and so in turn for these other epistemic instruments. Because there is no beginning, where would middle and end come from? To this extent your statement "the epistemic instruments are established by other epistemic instruments" is not adequate.

33. "These are established without the epistemic instruments"—your position is abandoned. There is an inequality to be explained, and you should state the special reason.

Then if you think "these epistemic instruments are established without epistemic instruments, but the objects to be known are established by the epistemic instruments," your position "objects are established by epistemic instruments" is abandoned. There is an inequality to be explained, since some objects are established by epistemic instruments, and some are not. You should state the special reason why some objects are established by epistemic instruments and some are not. As this is not specified, your supposition is not adequate.

At this point the opponent objects: "It is the very epistemic instruments which prove themselves as well as others. As it is said:

> As fire illuminates itself as well as others, so the epistemic instruments prove themselves and others.

As fire illuminates both itself and others, the epistemic instruments illuminate both themselves and others."

To this we reply:

34. This is a mistaken suggestion. For fire does not illuminate itself, as not perceiving it is not similar to the sight of a pot in the dark.

It is clearly a mistake to suggest that the epistemic instruments prove themselves and prove others, because fire does not illuminate itself. For if at first the pot in the dark, which is not illuminated by fire, is not perceived, it is perceived at a later time, being illuminated by fire. If there was first an unilluminated fire in the dark, which would be illuminated at a later time, then fire would illuminate itself. However, it is not like this. So far this assumption is not adequate. Moreover:

35. If, according to your assertion, fire illuminates itself like others, is it not also the case that fire consumes itself?

If, according to your assertion, as fire illuminates itself in the very same way as it illuminates other things, is it not also the case that it consumes itself in the very same way in which it consumes other things? However, it is not like this. In this context, the statement "fire illuminates itself in the same way in which it illuminates others" is not tenable. Moreover:

36. If, according to your assertion, fire illuminates both itself and others, darkness will conceal both itself and others, in the same way as fire.

If you thought fire proves both itself and others, would it not now be the case that the opposite thing, darkness, would also conceal both itself and others? But this is not observed. In this context your statement "fire illuminates both itself and others" is not tenable. Moreover:

37. There is no darkness in the blazing, nor in something else in which there is blazing. How does it do the illuminating, as illumination is the destruction of the dark?

Here there is no darkness in the fire and there is also no darkness where the fire is. Illumination is precisely the prevention of darkness. As far as darkness is not in the fire, and no darkness is where there is fire, which darkness does the fire prevent, and by the prevention of what does it illuminate both itself and others?

At this point the opponent objects: "As far as there is no darkness in the fire in this way, and as there is no darkness where there is fire, why does fire not illuminate both itself and others? For precisely the arising fire prevents darkness. As far as there is no darkness in the fire, and no darkness where there is fire, so far precisely the arising fire illuminates both itself and others." To this we reply:

38. "Precisely the arising fire illuminates"—this position is wrong. For that very arising fire does not connect with darkness.

The assertion that "precisely this arising fire illuminates itself and others" is not established. Why? For that very arising fire does not connect with darkness. Because of the lack of connection it does not destroy darkness, and because darkness is not prevented there is no illumination. Moreover:

39. But if an unconnected fire were to prevent darkness, the fire present here would prevent the darkness in all worlds.

If you think "an unconnected fire also prevents darkness," would it not be the case then that the fire present here right now will similarly prevent that unconnected darkness located in all worlds? But this is not what we observe. So far your asserting that "precisely the unconnected fire prevents darkness" is not tenable. Moreover:

40. If the epistemic instruments are self-established, the epistemic objects will be independent of the establishment of the epistemic instruments for you, for self-establishment is not dependent on anything else.

If you think "the epistemic instruments are self-established like fire," the establishment of the epistemic instruments will also be independent of the objects to be known. Why? Because what is self-established does not depend on anything else. Moreover, what is dependent is not self-established.

At this point the opponent objects, "If the epistemic instruments do not depend on the objects to be known, what is the problem?" To this we reply:

41. If for you the establishment of the epistemic instruments is independent of the objects to be known, then those will not be the epistemic instruments of anything.

If the establishment of the epistemic instruments is independent of the objects to be known, those epistemic instruments would not be the epistemic instruments of anything. This is the problem. Moreover, the epistemic instruments are epistemic instruments of something, therefore in this case the epistemic instruments are precisely not independent of the objects to be known.

42. Moreover, if one thought "the establishment of those is dependent," then what is the problem here? There would be the establishment of the established, because what is not established does not depend on another thing.

Moreover, if one also thought "the establishment of the epistemic instruments is dependent on the epistemic objects," in this case there is the establishment of the established fourfold epistemic instruments. Why? Since there is no dependence for an unestablished object. An unestablished Devadatta does not depend on any object. The establishment of the already established is not sensible; there is no making of what one has already made.

43. If the epistemic instruments are established dependent on the epistemic objects in every context, then the establishment of the epistemic objects is precisely not dependent on the epistemic instruments.

If the epistemic instruments are established dependent on the epistemic objects, then in this case the epistemic objects are not established dependent on the epistemic instruments. Why? For the thing to be established does not establish the instrument for establishing. And the epistemic instruments are said to be the instruments for establishing the epistemic objects. Moreover:

44. And if the establishment of the epistemic object is precisely independent of the epistemic instruments, what is achieved for you by establishing the epistemic instruments? Their purpose is already established.

If you think "the establishment of the epistemic objects is precisely independent of the epistemic instruments," what is achieved for you in this context by seeking the establishment of the epistemic instruments? Why? The epistemic objects, which are the purpose why one looks for the epistemic instruments, are established even without the epistemic instruments. What is to be achieved by the epistemic instruments in this case?

45. But then for you the establishment of the epistemic instruments is precisely dependent on the epistemic objects. This being so, instruments and epistemic objects are in fact reversed for you.

Moreover, if you think "the epistemic instruments are precisely dependent on the objects to be known, so there should not be the problem mentioned earlier," it follows that, instruments and epistemic objects being reversed for you, the epistemic instruments become epistemic objects because they are brought about by the epistemic objects, and the epistemic objects become epistemic instruments because they bring about the epistemic instruments.

46. Furthermore, if for you the establishment of the epistemic objects is by the epistemic instruments and the establishment of the epistemic instruments by the epistemic objects, neither is established for you.

Furthermore, if you think "the establishment of the epistemic objects is by the epistemic instruments because of the dependence on the epistemic instruments, and the establishment of the epistemic instruments is by the epistemic objects because of the dependence on the epistemic objects," neither is established for you. Why?

47. Because if these epistemic objects are established by precisely these epistemic instruments, and if these are to be established by the epistemic objects, how will they establish?

Because if these epistemic objects are established by the epistemic instruments, and if the epistemic instruments are to be established by precisely these epistemic objects, should we not ask how the unestablished epistemic objects will establish something, as the epistemic objects are unestablished, since their cause is unestablished?

48. And if these epistemic instruments are established by precisely these epistemic objects, and if these are to be established by the epistemic instruments, how will they establish?

And if these epistemic instruments are established by the epistemic objects, and if the epistemic objects are to be established by precisely these epistemic instruments, should we not ask how the unestablished epistemic instruments will establish something, as the epistemic instruments are unestablished, since their cause is unestablished?

49. If the son is to be produced by the father and if the father is to be produced by this very son, you have to say which produces which in this context.

If someone said "the son is to be produced by the father, and this father is to be produced by this very son," in this context you have to say now "which is to be produced by which." Just like this, you say "these very epistemic objects are to be established by the epistemic instruments, and, what is more, the epistemic instruments are to be established by those very objects." In this case now, which ones are to be established by which ones for you?

50. In this context, you should say which is the father and which is the son. Since both have the characteristic of father and son, this case is not clear to us.

Of the two just mentioned, father and son, which one is the father and which one is the son? Both have the characteristic of the father because they bring about something, and both have the characteristic of the son since they are brought about by something. In this case it is unclear to us which of the two is the father and which is the son. It is the very same with your instruments and epistemic objects: which of them are epistemic instruments and which are epistemic objects? For both are epistemic instruments because they establish something, and both are epistemic objects because they are to be established by something. In this case it is unclear to us which of these are epistemic instruments and which are epistemic objects.

51. The epistemic instruments are not self-established, nor are are they mutually established or established by other epistemic instruments, nor are they established by the epistemic objects or established without reason.

Perception is not self-established by that very perception, or inference by that very inference, or likeness by that very likeness, or testimony by that very testimony.

Perception is not established by something else, by inference, likeness, or testimony; inference by perception, likeness, or testimony; likeness by perception, inference, or testimony; testimony by perception, inference, or likeness.

It is also not the case that each one—perception, inference, likeness, or testimony—is established by another perception, inference, likeness, or testimony.

They are also not established by the epistemic objects either collectively or individually, included in their own field or in another. The epistemic instruments are also not established without a reason.

They are also not established by the collection of causes mentioned earlier, 20 or 30 or 40 or 26.

Your earlier statement, "because the things to be known are to be understood by the epistemic instruments, these things to be known exist as well as those epistemic instruments by which the things to be known are accessed" is not tenable. Concerning what you said earlier, "**7. People of who know the state of things think that auspicious phenomena have an auspicious substance. This distinction also holds for the other things,**" we reply:

52. If people who know the state of things speak of the auspicious things, the auspicious substance should be expressed in terms of a detailed division.

Those who know the state of things think that there is an auspicious substance of auspicious things, and this would have to be specified by you in terms of a detailed division: "This is the auspicious substance, these are the auspicious things, this is the consciousness of that auspicious thing, this is the substance of the consciousness of that auspicious thing." This would have to be done for all cases, but such a specification is not apparent. To this extent, your statement "the substance of things has been specified individually" is not tenable. Moreover:

53. And if the auspicious substance is produced based on conditions, how is this extrinsic nature of the auspicious things in fact a substance?

If the substance of the auspicious things is produced in dependence on the collection of causes and conditions, how can there be a substance of the auspicious things produced from an extrinsic nature? It is just the same for the inauspicious things, and so forth. In this context, your statement "the auspicious substance of the auspicious things was explained, as was the inauspicious substance, etc., of the inauspicious things, and so forth" is not tenable. Moreover:

54. If the substance of the auspicious things was not produced in dependence on anything, there would be no religious practice.

Furthermore, you might think "the auspicious substance of the auspicious things is not produced in dependence on anything, nor is the inauspicious substance of the inauspicious things, nor the indeterminate substance of the indeterminate things. Therefore there is no religious practice." Why? Because this is the denial of dependent origination. And because dependent origination is denied, the apprehension of dependent origination is denied. This is because an apprehension of non-existent dependent origination cannot be obtained. And when there is no apprehension of dependent origination, there is no apprehension of the true state of things. For the Blessed One said, "O Monks, whoever sees dependent origination sees the true state of things." Because there is no apprehension of the true state of things, there is no religious practice.

On the other hand, one might argue for the same conclusion by saying that the denial of dependent origination entails the denial of the origin of suffering, as dependent origination is the origin of suffering. Because the origin of suffering is denied, suffering is denied. While there is no origin, from where will suffering arise? Because suffering and its origin are denied, the cessation of suffering is denied. While there is no origin of suffering, the destruction of what will be its cessation? While there is no cessation of suffering, what is to be obtained on a path that leads to the cessation of suffering? In this way the four noble truths do not exist. While these do not exist there is no fruit of religious practice, since this fruit is obtained by the apprehension of these truths. Because there are no such fruits, there is no religious practice. Moreover:

55. There would be neither right nor wrong nor worldly conventions. They would be permanent and substantial; because they are permanent they are acausal.

While it is like this, which fault follows for you from the negation of dependent origination? "There is no right, there is no wrong, there are no worldly conventions." Why? Because as this is all dependently originated, when there is no dependent origination where should it come from? Also, what is substantial would not be dependently originated, but acausal and permanent. Why? Because acausal things are permanent. In this context, the non-existence of religious practice would follow exactly. And there is a contradiction with your own position. Why? Because the Blessed One said that all compounded things are impermanent. Hence they are permanent because they are substantially permanent.

56. Thus there is a difficulty for the inauspicious things, the indeterminate ones, those leading to liberation, and so forth. To this extent everything compounded is just not compounded for you.

The method which has been indicated with reference to the auspicious things is just the same for the inauspicious, for the indeterminate, for those leading to liberation, and so forth. To this extent, for you everything compounded becomes not compounded. Why? While there is no cause there is no arising, remaining, and decay. Because there is no characteristic of the compounded, in the absence of arising, remaining, and decay everything compounded becomes uncompounded. In this context, your statement "because auspicious things and so forth are endowed with substance, all things fail to be empty" is not tenable.

Concerning what you said earlier, "**9. And if there was no substance, there would also not even be the name 'insubstantiality of things,' for there is no name without referent,**" we reply:

57. Where someone said "a name has a referent," one would say "then substance exists." You have to reply "we do not assert a name of this kind."

Where someone said "a name has a referent," one would say "then substance exists." You have to reply: "If there is a referring name of a substance it has to exist due to the substantial referent. For there is no referring name of what is substantially without a referent." However, we do not assert a referring name. This is because a name, too, due to the absence of substance in things, is insubstantial and therefore empty. Because of its emptiness it is non-referring. In this context, your statement "because of being endowed with a name there is a substantial referent" is not tenable.

58. The name "non-existent"—what is this, something existent or again something non-existent? For if it is existent or if it is nonexistent, either way your position is deficient.

And this name "non-existent," is that existent or non-existent? For if it is the name of an existent, or if it is the name of a non-existent, in both cases the thesis is deficient. If in this context the name "non-existent" is the name of an existent, to that extent the thesis is abandoned. For it is not the case that something is now non-existent, now existent. Moreover, if the name "non-existent" is the name of a non-existent—there is no name of something which does not exist. To that extent, the thesis "the name exists substantially, so there is a substantial referent of the name," is deficient. Moreover:

59. The emptiness of all things was presented earlier. To this extent, this is a criticism of a non-thesis.

The emptiness of all things was presented here in detail by our earlier remarks. The emptiness of the name has been asserted above, as well. Having adopted the non-emptiness of things, you replied to this "if the substance of things did not exist there would be no name 'non-substance.'" So far your criticism amounts to a criticism of a non-thesis, because we do not say that there is a referring name.

Concerning what you said earlier, "**10. Rather, substance exists, yet the substance of things does not exist. It has to be explained to what this thingless substance belongs,**" we reply to this:

60. "Substance exists and it is not a substance of things"—the worry expressed there is no worry.

This is because we do not negate the substance of things, or assert the substance of some object distinct from things. While this is so, is not that your criticism "if things are without substance, now the substance of which other object distinct from things is there? It would be right if this was pointed out" disappears from view and is in fact no criticism at all.

Concerning what you said earlier, "**11. To the extent to which the negation 'there is no pot in the house' is precisely a negation of an existent, your negation is a negation of an existing substance,**" we reply to this:

61. If negation is of an existent thing, is it not that emptiness is established? Because you negate the insubstantiality of things.

If negation is of an existent thing and not of a non-existent one, and if you negate the insubstantiality of all things, is it not that the insubstantiality of all things is established? Your speech, which is a negation, establishes emptiness because it is the negation of the insubstantiality of all things.

62. Or, if you negate emptiness and that emptiness does not exist, is your statement that "negation is of an existent thing" then not abandoned?

Or, if you negate the insubstantiality and emptiness of all things, and if that emptiness does not exist, now in that case your thesis that "negation is of an existing thing, not of a non-existing thing" is abandoned. Moreover:

63. I do not negate anything, and there is nothing to be negated. To this extent you misrepresent me when you say "you negate."

If I negated anything, then what you said would be appropriate. But I do not negate anything, since there is not anything to be negated. Therefore, while all things are empty, while the object of negation and the negation do not exist, you introduce a misrepresentation by saying "you negate."

Concerning what you said earlier, "**12. Now as this substance does not exist, what is negated by that statement of yours? For the negation of a non-existent is accomplished without speech,**" we reply to this:

64. Regarding your assertion that "expressing the negation of a non-existent object is accomplished without speech": in our case speech makes the non-existent known, it does not refute it.

When you say "the negation of a non-existent is also accomplished without speech," what does your statement "all things are insubstantial" do?' We reply: indeed, this statement "all things are insubstantial" does not make all things insubstantial. Nevertheless, while there is no substance, it makes known that "things are insubstantial."

In the same way, suppose someone said, while Devadatta is absent from the house, "Devadatta is in the house," and someone would reply, "he is not." That statement does not bring about the non-existence of Devadatta, but it only makes the absence of Devadatta in the house known. Likewise, that statement "there is no substance of things" does not bring about the insubstantiality of things, nevertheless it makes the absence of substance in all things known.

Moreover, all things lack substance, like an illusory person. Because they are ignorant of the lack of a real core in persons, stupid and ignorant childish beings superimpose a substance onto them. If there is no substance, the non-existence of substance is definitely established even without words or excluding words, because words bring about the understanding that things lack substance.

In this context, your earlier statement "when there is no substance, what does that statement 'there is no substance' do? The absence of substance is also established without words" is not tenable. And, in addition: "**13. As ignorant people wrongly perceive water in a mirage, in the same way there would be a wrong perception for you in this case, for a non-existent object is negated. Etc.**" Again, we reply to the four verses 13–16 you gave by saying:

65. By the example of the mirage, you once again brought up an important discussion. In this context, too, you should listen to the demonstration of how this example is suitable.

You once again brought up a great discussion by the example of the mirage. In this context, too, the demonstration of how this example is suitable should be heard.

66. If perception existed substantially, it would not be dependently produced. The perception which is dependent, however, is it not precisely emptiness?

If the perception of water in a mirage was substantial, it would not be dependently originated. As far as it is produced dependent on the mirage, dependent on the mistaken vision, and dependent on the irregular mental activity, it is dependently arisen. And because it is dependently arisen, therefore it is empty of substance. It is as was said earlier. Moreover:

67. If perception existed substantially, who would remove the perception? As far as the same pattern applies to the remaining cases this is a non-criticism.

If the perception of water in the mirage existed substantially, who exactly would remove it? This is because substance, like the heat of fire, the wetness of water, the spaciousness of space, cannot be removed. But its removal is perceived. So far perception is empty of substance. Similarly, it has to be understood clearly that the same procedure applies to the remaining cases as well, the five beginning with the object perceived. In this context, your statement "because there is the set of six all things are not empty" is not tenable.

Concerning what you said earlier, "**17. Your reason is not established. Because there is no substance, where then does your reason come from? Moreover, no matter is established without a reason,**" we reply:

68. Because the case is the same, the difficulty of the absence of the reason, which was noted in the discussion of the method for refuting the example of the mirage, has already been answered by this.

Now the difficulty of the absence of the reason is to be understood as answered as well by this earlier discussion. This is because the very discussion brought up in the earlier reason of the negation of the set of six is also to be considered here.

Concerning what you said earlier, "**20. Supposing that the negation is earlier and the negated later fails to be successful. And being later and being simultaneous fail to be successful. Therefore substance exists,**" we reply:

69. Because the case is the same, the difficulty of the reason in the three times has already been answered by this. The proponent of emptiness obtains the counter-reason of the three times.

It has to be understood that the issue of expressing the negation in the three time was answered earlier. Why? Because of the fallacy of the same predicament. As far as according to your statement the negation is not achieved in the three times, the object of negation is like the negation. While negation and object of negation do not exist you cannot maintain that "the negation is negated." The very reason of the assertion of the negation of the three times is obtained by the proponents of emptiness, and not by you, since they are negators of the substance of all things.

Alternatively, it is answered by what was said earlier: "**63. I do not negate anything, and there is nothing to be negated. To this extent you misrepresent me when you say 'you negate.'**"

Then you may think "negation is established in the three times as well. The cause is seen at the time before, as well as at the time after, as well as at the same time. In this case, the cause at the time before is like the father of the son; at the time after, it is like the student of the teacher; and at the same time, it is like the illumination of the lamp."

We reply: It is not like that. This is because this manner of proceeding contains the three difficulties mentioned earlier.

Moreover, if you arrive in this way at the existence of the negation, your thesis is abandoned. The negation of substance is established by this method.

70. For whom there is emptiness, there are all things. For whom there is no emptiness there is nothing whatsoever.

For whom there is emptiness there are all natural and supernatural things. Why? For whom there is emptiness there is dependent origination. For whom there is dependent origination there are the four noble truths. For whom there are the four noble truths there are the fruits of religious practice, and all the special attainments. For whom there are all the special attainments there are the three jewels, the Buddha, the Dharma, and the Sangha.

For whom there is dependent origination there is righteousness, its cause, and its result, as well as unrighteousness, its cause, and its result. For whom there is the righteous and the unrighteous, their cause and their result there are the obscurations, their origin, and their bases.

For whom there is all this, the law of the fortunate and unfortunate states of rebirth, the attainment of the fortunate and unfortunate states of rebirth, the way of going toward the fortunate and unfortunate states of rebirth, the passing beyond the fortunate and unfortunate states of rebirth, the means for passing beyond the fortunate and unfortunate states of rebirth as well as all worldly conventions are established.

It is to be understood by each one for himself according to this instruction; only some of it can be taught verbally.

Once more:

I venerate the one who taught emptiness, dependent origination, and the middle way as one thing, the incomparable Buddha.

This is the end of the verses of the Venerable Nāgārjuna, who composed the 450 verses. It was written down by the noble Dharmakīrti in the way he obtained it, for the sake of all sentient beings.

3

Commentary

Veneration to the Buddha!

While the Sanskrit manuscript of the *Vigrahavyāvartanī* opens with the praise of the Buddha, the Tibetan translation begins with an invocation of Mañjuśrī Kumārabhūta, the customary way of starting a text dealing with material belonging to the genre of the Perfection of Wisdom (*prajñāpāramitā*). These homages are not part of the text proper, however, but have been added the by the scribes or translators. The *Vigrahavyāvartanī* begins straightaway with a philosophical argument. Candrakīrti argues that the reason why the *Vigrahavyāvartanī*, unlike many other works of Nāgārjuna, does not start with a praise of the Buddha is that it is a mere elaboration (*'phros pa*) of Nāgārjuna's exposition of Madhyamaka expounded elsewhere and should therefore not be conceived of as an independent treatise in need of such a dedication.[1]

3.1 The Status of the Theory of Emptiness [1–4, 21–29]

3.1.1 The Madhyamaka Dilemma [1–2, 21–24]

1. If the substance of all things is not to be found anywhere, your assertion which is devoid of substance is not able to refute substance.

1. *dbu ma las 'phros pa ste / rang gi rgyud gud na med pas logs shig tu bstod pa ma brjod de* (Loizzo 2007: 242:1–2).

With his first objection, the opponent raises a point at the very heart of Madhyamaka thinking: the status of the Mādhyamika's own statement of his theory. The sophistication of this objection underlines the fact that the *Vigrahavyāvartanī* was not meant to be an expository text and was composed later than Nāgārjuna's *Mūlamadhyamakakārikā*, his main work outlining the theory of emptiness. The *Vigrahavyāvartanī* was intended for an audience already familiar with Nāgārjuna's theses looking for a discussion of potential difficulties and objections.

The "assertion" the opponent has in mind is the central Madhyamaka thesis that everything is empty. As a universal claim, it subsumes the statement "everything is empty" under it. The opponent wants to argue that the emptiness of this statement somehow undermines its argumentative force.

If the substance of things was not found anywhere, in the causes, in the conditions, or in the combination of the causes and the conditions, and if it is also not separate from these, it is said: "all things are empty."

For the sprout does not exist in the seed which is its cause; it does not exist in each one of earth, water, fire, wind, and so forth, which are agreed to be its conditions; it does not exist in the combinations of conditions, nor in the combination of causes and conditions, and it does also not exist as separate from these, free from causes and conditions.

As substance does not exist anywhere here, the sprout is without substance, and since it is without substance it is empty. As this sprout without substance is empty because of its lack of substance, in the same way all things are empty as well because of their lack of substance.

Here the opponent outlines one of the standard arguments for the Madhyamaka thesis of universal emptiness based on the notion of causation. This, as well as other causation-based arguments for emptiness are described in chapter 2 of Nāgārjuna's *Mūlamadhyamakakārikā*.[2] The example considered here is that of the sprout of some plant, the effect, which is brought about by a cause, the seed. The seed on its own is, of course, unable to bring about a sprout; it has to be assisted by a collection of background conditions or a causal field, comprising among other things soil, water, nutrients, light, and so forth. All of these can be regarded as compounds of the "four great elements," earth, water, fire, and wind, which according to the Abhidharma constitute the basis of all physical phenomena.

The argument for emptiness under consideration now investigates the relationship between the the effect and the cause and conditions that bring it about. The sprout is not already present in the seed: if we take the seed apart we will

2. For a more detailed analysis of these see Westerhoff (2009a, chapter 5: 91–127).

find no sprout, and the seed on its own, devoid of the causal field; will never bring forth a sprout. Needless to say, we also will not find a sprout in parts of the causal field (the soil, water, and so forth), nor in collections of some of them, nor in a collection of all of them put together. If we add the seed to the causal field, there is still no sprout to be found: the cause and causal field together bring about the effect, but do not contain it tucked away somewhere inside them. Part of what we mean by "*a* causes *b*" is that the cause *a* first exists without *b* and then, at a subsequent later moment, brings forth the effect. For this reason, *b* cannot be part of *a*, since the parts of an object are simultaneous with it.

When the argument claims that the effect is not separate from the cause and conditions, this does not deny that the sprout is a thing which we can clearly distinguish from other things, such as the seed, the soil, water, and so forth. It rather makes a claim of *existential dependence*: if the seed, soil, water, and so forth (the cause and causal field) had not existed, the sprout (the effect) would not have existed, either, in the same way in which I would not have existed if my father had not, or the Koh-i-Noor would not have existed if there had been no carbon in the universe.

But if two objects are different substances or composites of different substances, it should be possible to give a clear analysis of their identity or difference: either they are identical, share a part, one is included within the other, or they are distinct. None of these possibilities applies to the seed and the sprout: they are not the same, they do not overlap, the cause does not include the effect as a part, and they are also not different substances, since it is an essential part of the meaning of "substance" that substances do not depend on other things. Having drawn a blank in evaluating all of the theoretical possibilities, the Madhyamaka arrives at the conclusion that there must have been something wrong with our presuppositions. The assumption that cause and effect exist as distinct substances had led to a problem and is therefore given up. Both are empty of substancehood, and since everything depends on causes and conditions, the Madhyamaka infers the general conclusion that everything is empty of substance.[3]

Here we say: If it is like this, your assertion, which claims that "all things are empty," is also empty. Why? Because your assertion does not exist in the cause: it does not exist in the great elements collectively or individually.

It does also not exist in the conditions which are the action of the chest, the throat, the lips, the tongue, the root of the teeth, the palate, the nose, the head and so forth; it

3. Nāgārjuna does not discuss the status of entities often regarded as being outside of the causal framework, such as mathematical objects. Some passages in his works might be interpreted as a denial of abstract objects altogether. Alternatively, we could understand the logical entailment between mathematical concepts as a dependence relation, so that mathematical objects as the relata of a dependence relation could not be substances, either. See Westerhoff (2009a, 112, note 61, 203).

does not exist in the combination of the causes and the conditions; and it also does not exist as separate from this, free from the combination of causes and conditions. Since it does not exist anywhere among these, it is without substance. Since it is without substance, it is empty. For this reason it is impossible that it dispels the substance of all things.

The Madhyamaka says all things are empty, and, as the opponent rightly points out, the statement "all things are empty" is a thing itself. Note that the statement is here regarded as a token, not a type. The opponent refers to a timed event, which is the utterance of the statement "all things are empty," not to what is expressed by different utterances of this statement (the statement-type). Statements as tokens are evidently causally produced in the same way as sprouts, though by different causes and conditions: instead of a seed, soil, water, and so forth, they require the combined action of the various production-places of speech as described in traditional Indian phonetics.[4] If sprouts are empty, statements are empty, too, and if all statements are empty, so is each particular one of them. Why is this a problem for the Madhyamaka?

Why? This is because a non-existent fire cannot burn, a non-existent knife cannot cut, a non-existent water cannot moisten. In the same way, a non-existent assertion cannot negate the substance of all things. Therefore your statement that the substance of all things has been negated everywhere, that the substance of things has been dispelled everywhere, is not tenable.

The opponent here understands Nāgārjuna's term "empty" to mean "non-existent." Rather than taking "*x* is empty" as "*x* does not exist substantially," he understands it as "*x* does not exist at all." And of course non-existent things are not causally efficacious: the non-existent ten-pound note in my pocket cannot buy anything. Nāgārjuna's position is therefore argumentationally impotent: the thesis of universal emptiness cannot refute any philosophical position, since it does not even exist.

This understanding also equates Nāgārjuna's theory with a form of nihilism: if everything is empty and if "empty" means "does not exist," then nothing whatsoever exists. Not only is the thesis of universal emptiness unable to refute the opponent's position, there is no position to be refuted, since the opponent's position also does not exist.

REPLY

21. If my speech is not in the combination of causes and conditions and also not distinct from them, is it not the case that emptiness is established because of the absence of the substance of things?

4. On this see Allen (1953). Tucci (1929: 23–24) mentions a parallel passage in a work attributed to Vasubandhu.

If my speech is not in the cause, not among the great elements, neither in the collection of conditions nor distinct from it, if it is not in the action of the chest, the throat, the lips, the root of the teeth, the palate, the nose, the head, and so forth, if it is not in the combination of those, is not free from the combination of causes and conditions, not distinct from them—to this extent it is without substance, and because it is without substance it is empty. Thus is it not the case that the emptiness of my speech is established because of its lack of substance? And as the speech of mine is empty because of the lack of substance, so all things are also empty because of the lack of substance.

Nāgārjuna agrees with the initial part of the opponent's objection. The thesis of universal emptiness is indeed so universal that it includes itself. As was indicated by the opponent, the token statement "all things are empty" is a specific sound-event produced in dependence on causes and conditions and therefore empty of substance for the same reason that other things such as the causally produced sprout are empty.

In this context, your statement "The emptiness of all things is not established because of the emptiness of your speech" is not tenable.

22. ***The dependent existence of things is said to be emptiness, for what is dependently existent is lacking substance.***

You do not understand the meaning of the emptiness of things. Not knowing the meaning of emptiness, you formulate the following criticism: "The negation of the substance of things is not established because of the emptiness of your speech." In this context, the dependent existence of things is emptiness. Why? Because of insubstantiality. Those things which are dependently arisen are not endowed with substance, because there is no substance. Why? Because of the dependence on causes and conditions. If things existed substantially they would exist without causes and conditions; however, they do not exist in this way. Therefore they are said to be without substance, and because they are without substance, empty. Therefore it follows that in the same way my own speech is without substance, because it is dependently arisen, and because it is without substance it is empty.

Where Nāgārjuna disagrees with his opponent is when it comes to the implications of accepting that the thesis of universal emptiness is empty, too. The opponent takes this to mean that the thesis in question does not exist, and is therefore unable to do any work in an argument. This, however, implies a mistaken understanding of Nāgārjuna's use of the term "empty." When he says something is "empty of substance," he does not mean to say that this something does not exist, but that it is dependently arisen, causally produced in dependence on causes and conditions.[5] The existence of substances implies that they are at

5. "Empty" does not mean "non-existent"; it does also not mean "false." This would mean that Nāgārjuna's thesis of universal emptiness entailed the liar paradox. On this, see Mabbett (1996), Sagal (1992).

the bottom of the chain of dependence relations. Other things can depend on them, but they cannot depend on other things. But a causally produced thing cannot be at the bottom of such a chain, since it in turn depends for its existence on the cause which brought it into being. And since reference to causally produced objects essentially involves reference to causality, a causally originated object cannot exist substantially if the causal relation is to be understood as conceptually constructed. Given the Buddhist theory of momentariness, according to which objects only exist during a temporally minimal moment, it has to be understood as so constructed. Causality relates cause and effect which exist at different times; we can only squeeze one of these relata into the present moment, so the other must be supplied by our mind, either as a memory or as an expectation. The causal relation must therefore be understood as brought about by the mind, not as something existing mind-independently in the world out there.[6] For this reason, causally produced things cannot be substances. "Being empty" and "being dependently arisen" refer to the same property, namely, the absence of substance.[7]

Nāgārjuna illustrates this by an example:

For instance a chariot, pot, cloth, and so forth, which are empty of substance because they are dependently originated, perform in their respective ways by removing wood, grass, earth, by containing honey, water, or milk, and by bringing forth protection against cold, wind, or heat. Similarly my speech, which is also without substance because it is dependently arisen, plays a part in establishing the lack of substance of things. In this context, the statement "Because of the absence of substance there is the emptiness of your statement, and because of the emptiness of that statement it fails to accomplish the negation of the substance of all things" is not tenable.

If emptiness does not entail non-existence but refers to the fact that objects stand in existential dependence relations to other objects, it is quite clear that emptiness does not preclude functional efficacy. Even though a chariot is dependently originated, being existentially dependent on its parts, and causally dependent on whatever brought the parts into existence, this does not mean that one cannot use it to transport wood or other goods. In fact, as Nāgārjuna remarks elsewhere, it is the very fact that objects like the chariot are mereologically and causally dependent in this way that allows them to fulfill their specific function.[8] The very same is true of Nāgārjuna's thesis of universal emptiness. Even though it is as empty as everything else, this does not imply that it is not capable of playing a role in arguments.

6. For a further discussion of this point, see Siderits (2004).
7. *Mūlamadhyamakakārikā* 24: 18.
8. *Mūlamadhyamakakārikā* 1:10, Garfield (1995: 119).

*23. **Suppose one artificial being were to hinder another artificial being, or an illusory man would hinder one brought about by his own illusionistic power. This negation would be just like that.***

This point requires some explanation. First, we have to note that the verbal root *prati-ṣidh* employed here can mean both "to prevent" or "to restrain someone from doing something" as well as "to negate." In the original text, the parallelism between one man keeping another one from doing something and one statement keeping another from holding is much more pronounced than in our translation, as there is no English verb covering both meanings.

It would be as if an artificial man hindered another artificial man[9] *engaged in some action or as if an illusory man brought forth by an illusionist would hinder another illusory man engaged in some action who was brought forth by the illusory man's own illusory power. In this case the artificial man who is hindered is empty, as is the one who hinders him. The illusory man who is hindered is empty, as is the one who hinders him.*

This is the first of several references to illusionistic performances found in the *Vigrahavyāvartanī*. It is not easy to determine the nature of the specific example Nāgārjuna had in mind here, although the general idea is clear enough. We cannot be quite sure what exactly the difference between the "artificial man" (*nirmitakaḥ*) and the "illusory man" (*māyā-puruṣaḥ*) is supposed to amount to. Perhaps they both name a phantom created by an illusionist, or perhaps an automaton created by non-magical feats of engineering is meant by one or both of the terms.[10] For the philosophical point this passage is trying to make, it is not important whether we conceive of the illusory persons as phantoms conjured up by a magician, as automata, or even as characters in a film. It is important, though, to be aware that Nāgārjuna mentions two different examples here. In the first one an artificial creature keeps another one from doing something. The second is somewhat more intricate, as it involves two layers of illusion.[11]

9. The Sanskrit reads here *puruṣam abhyāpataṃ* "a man who came along" (Yonezawa 2008:256:4), which the Tibetan renders as *sprul pa'i skyes bu*. Our translation here follows the Tibetan, since it is clear from verse 23 that this second man is supposed to be artificial as well.

10. Warder (1980: 368) renders *māyā-puruṣa* as "puppet." The more usual term for such automata would be *yantra*. Such *yantrāni* are occasionally referred to in the Buddhist literature as illustrations of illusory existents, for example in the *Pañcaviṃśatisāhasrikā Prajñāpāramitāsūtra* (Dutt 1934:186:15–17); for more references, see Raghavan (1956: 5–6). The *Laṅkāvatārasūtra* in particular refers to a *yantra-puruṣa* (Nanjio 1923: 94:15); unfortunately the exact nature of this device is not specified.

11. This example is also used by Nāgārjuna in a different context in two other places. In *Mūlamadhyamakakārikā* 17: 31–32, we read: "It is as if the teacher were to form an artificial man by his magical powers and this artificial man were to form another artificial man: in the same way the agent is like the artificial man formed, and his action like the other artificial man formed by the first" *yathā nirmitakaṃ śāstā nirmimīta rddhisaṃpadā / nirmito nirmimītānyaṃ sa ca nirmitakaḥ punaḥ // tathā nirmitakākāraḥ kartā yat karma tat kṛtam / tadyathā nirmitenānyo nirmito nirmitas tathā.*

First an illusionist creates an illusion, and then this illusion (apparently itself endowed with illusionistic powers) creates another illusion and keeps it from doing something. The key difference between these two cases is that in the first the "hindering" happens between beings at the same level of unreality, whereas in the second the hindered is one level less real than the hinderer, since he is an illusion's illusion.

Both cases can easily be given a cinematic analogue. In the first case, imagine two men in a film, one keeping the other from opening a door. In the second, imagine a real man, making a film about a man making a film. The second man then projects his film-in-a-film on a wall and, just before the climax, switches off the projector. He has just hindered the illusion's illusion (the man in the film-in-the-film) from doing something.

Therefore in just the same way the negation of the substance of all things is established by my empty speech. In this context, your statement "The negation of the substance of all things is not established by your speech because of its emptiness" is not tenable. The discussion in six points mentioned by you is also refuted by this. Indeed, while it is like that my speech does not fail to be included among all things. There is nothing non-empty, also it is not the case that all things are non-empty.

Unfortunately, Nāgārjuna does not explain in detail how the examples of illusory men apply to the case of his empty thesis of universal emptiness. Nevertheless, in the case of the first example this is clear enough. Like the two men in the film, Nāgārjuna's thesis of universal emptiness and the opponent's postulation of a substance exist at the same ontological level. They are both empty of substance, as both men are only men in a film. It is for this reason that they can interact; a cinematic man could not keep a real man from opening a door. Therefore Nāgārjuna's thesis of universal emptiness has the power to refute the opponent's assertion of substance.

Tola and Dragonetti misunderstand the point made here when they claim that "the argument adduced against the opponent is very weak because, if a man a or a thing created by magic, and as such without an own being [i.e., without substance], is efficient, hence it does not inevitably follow that all beings

---

The *Śūnyatāsaptati* 40–41 (Tola and Dragonetti 1987) states that "Just as the Tathāgata creates an illusion by his illusionistic powers, and this illusion creates another illusion in turn, in that case the Tathāgata's illusion is empty, not to speak of the illusion's illusion. If something which is a mere conceptual construction is admitted, both these two are existent" *ji ltar bcom ldan de bzhin gshegs/ de ni rdzu 'phrul gyis sprul pa/ sprul pa mdzad la sprul des kyang/ sprul pa gzhan zhig sprul par byed// de la de bzhin gshegs sprul stong/ sprul pas sprul pa smos ci dgos/ rtog pa tsam gang ci yang rung/ de dag gnyi ga yod pa yin*. Note, however, that both these usages of the example serve to illustrate the other direction of the mutual implication of emptiness and causal efficiency. Rather than showing how empty objects can participate in causal contexts, they illustrate how the elements in a causal chain connecting agent and action can be empty.

and things without an own being are efficient."[12] First, it is not true that all insubstantial things are efficient: a hare's horn or a square circle are without substance and unable to act as members in a causal chain. Second it is the opponent who made the universal claim that all things without substance lack causal efficiency. In this case, the production of a single counterexample, such as that of the artificially created man who forms part of a causal chain, would be sufficient to refute it.

The point of the second example, where an illusory magician prevents his own creation from doing something, is less clear. What might be meant is the following. Later Madhyamaka literature stresses the point that our conception of substance is something wrongly superimposed on a world of phenomena that really lacks it.[13] To that extent, thinking that there are substances out there in the world is like a magician beholding his own creation: even though it appears to him to have external existence, it is really a projection of his own mind, something he himself brought about. (The magician himself, by the way, is illusory because our notion of a person who superimposes substance onto the world is also just a superimposition on a disparate and changing set of physico-psychological elements). Therefore when we negate the existence of substance, we are really negating something that our mistaken projection brought into the world in the first place. To this extent we are like a magician trying dissolve the phantoms he himself called into existence.

The "discussion in six points" is set out by the opponent in his next objection.

2. *Moreover, if that statement exists substantially, your earlier thesis is refuted. There is an inequality to be explained, and the specific reason for this should be given.*

We now see that the opponent in fact presents Nāgārjuna with a dilemma. The first horn was described in verse 1 ("all things are empty and the thesis of universal emptiness is empty too"), the second ("all things are empty apart from the thesis of universal emptiness") is given here. If Nāgārjuna does not want to regard his own thesis as empty, he has to argue that for some reason the thesis of universal emptiness does not apply to itself. But then he would have to supply a reason for this inequality, as *prima facie* the thesis is an object like all other objects.

Moreover, you could think that there should not be this mistake by arguing, "This statement exists substantially and because it is a substance it is not empty. Therefore it negates the substance of all things, dispels the substance of all things." We say in reply: If it is like this, your earlier thesis that all things are empty is refuted.

12. Tola and Dragonetti (1998: 155).

13. The term used for such a superimposition is *samāropa*. Nāgārjuna only uses it once, in *Mūlamadhyamakakārikā* 16:10. Candrakīrti discusses this in greater detail; see for example the *Prasannapadā* (La Vallée Poussin 1903–1913:347:1–3). Some further discussion is in Tanji (2000: 352, 355), and Tillemans (2001).

As the opponent rightly notes, if Nāgārjuna regards his own statement as exempt from the thesis of universal emptiness, this implies that it cannot be strictly true, since it is not truly universal. It does not apply to all phenomena but only to a special collection, that is, to everything apart from the thesis of universal emptiness. So even if Nāgārjuna manages to provide a reason for why his own thesis is not empty, he can only argue that a large, though not all-comprehending, set of objects is empty.

Furthermore, your statement is also included in all things. How can it be that while all things are empty your assertion by which, because of its non-emptiness, the substance of all things is negated is not empty? Thus a controversy involving six points ensues. How again is this?

1. *Look, if all things are empty, this implies that your statement is empty too because it is included among all things. Because of that emptiness, the negation fails to be accomplished. Therefore the negation "all things are empty" fails to be accomplished.*
2. *If, however, the negation "all things are empty" is accomplished, this implies that your assertion is also not empty. Because of the non-emptiness the negation fails to be accomplished by this.*[14]

This is just a repetition of the first horn of the dilemma. If emptiness implies non-existence, the thesis of universal emptiness is argumentationally impotent. On the other hand, if the thesis *is* able to function in an argument, then it cannot be empty (since, on the opponent's understanding of "empty," this would mean that it is non-existent), because non-existent things cannot fulfil a function. Because of its own non-emptiness, the negation of the substance of *all* things fails to be accomplished. At best the substance of some things is refuted, but not that of the thesis of universal emptiness.

3. *But if all things are empty and your assertion, by which the negation is achieved, is not empty, this implies that your assertion is not included among all things. There is a contradiction by the example.*

The "example" the opponent has in mind here is the statement "all things are empty" which, for the sake of embracing the second horn of the dilemma, is considered to be not empty.

4. *If, however, your assertion is included among all things, if all things are empty, this implies that your assertion is also empty. And because it is empty it cannot accomplish a negation.*

14. The translation here follows the Chinese translation, which appears to me to make most philosophical sense. It is hard to understand the meaning of this passage as given in the Sankskrit, while the Tibetan just reiterates the argument formulated in the preceding point. See Bhattacharya et al. (1978: 44, note 3; 96–97, note 4).

5. *Then, assume your assertion was empty and by it the negation "everything is empty" was established. But in that case all empty things would be causally efficacious, and this is not admissible.*

That empty things *are* causally efficacious is of course exactly what Nāgārjuna wants to assert, as he makes clear in verse 22. He can do so because, unlike the opponent, he does not intend "empty" to mean "non-existent" but rather "dependently arisen."

6. *Assume then that all things are empty and lack causal efficacy, and let there be no contradiction by the example. Having assumed this, however, your empty assertion fails to accomplish the negation of the substance of all things.*

Furthermore, because your statement exists, there is an inequality as a consequence: some things are empty, some things are not empty. And while there is such an inequality, it is necessary to give the specific reason by which something would be empty or not empty. That, however, has not been specified. In this context, your statement "all things are empty" is not tenable.

The unsatisfactory consequences of embracing either horn of the dilemma are described once more. If the thesis of universal emptiness is non-existent and therefore lacking causal efficiency, it cannot be of much use in refuting the opponent's position. But since the thesis manifestly does exist, it cannot be true, since not *everything* is empty and therefore non-existent. Moreover, Nāgārjuna has not indicated what distinguishes the thesis of universal emptiness from all other things, so that we might be able to argue that unlike them it alone is not empty.

REPLY

24. This speech does not exist substantially, therefore there is no destruction of my position. There is no inequality, and no particular reason to be mentioned.

So far, since my speech is dependently originated it is not established substantially. As was said before, because it is not substantially established it is empty. As far as my speech is empty and all the other things are also empty, there is no inequality. If we say "this speech is not empty, yet all the other things are empty," there would be an inequality. But it is not like this and therefore there is no inequality.

And as far as the inequality of us saying "that speech is not empty; however, all the other things are empty" does not arise, to that extent we do not have to give the special reason as in, "by this reason that speech is not empty, however, all things are empty."

In this context, your statement "there is the destruction of your thesis, there is an inequality, and you should state the special reason" is not tenable.

Nāgārjuna makes it clear that he does not want to embrace the second horn of the dilemma. The thesis of universal emptiness applies to itself, that is, it is included among all things. When Nāgārjuna says "all things are empty," "all" means "all," not "all of a particular kind, excluding some others." For this reason, there is no need to look for a specific difference that sets this thesis apart from all other things and gives it a special ontological status in order to justify a restricted version of the thesis of universal emptiness. Nāgārjuna does not attempt a move analogous to the attempt of dissolving the antinomy of the set of all sets by claiming that such a set is no set but a proper class.[15] No attempt to move the thesis of universal emptiness into a category of its own, "one level higher up," is made.

It is also evident how the example of illusion presented in verse 23 refutes the above discussion in six points. For the dilemma described there reduces to the simple charge of argumentational impotence once the second horn has been rejected. And the example of illusion is meant precisely as an illustration of how empty objects can still fulfill functions, so that there is no tension between the thesis of universal emptiness being itself empty and its ability to refute the opponent's assertion of substance.[16]

From a comparative perspective, it is interesting to note that the criticism presented in verses 1–2 has recently resurfaced again in the debates about global relativism (or global antirealism). Paul Boghossian notes that:

> the global relativist is caught on the horns of a dilemma. Either he intends his own view to be absolutely true, or he intends it to be only relatively true, true relative to some theory or other. If the former, he refutes himself, for he would then have admitted at least one absolute truth. If the latter, we may just ignore him, for then it is just a report of what the relativist finds agreeable to say.[17]

Of course, it would be both anachronistic as well as systematically unsatisfactory to equate Nāgārjuna's theory with the global relativism of the Rortyan variety Boghossian has in mind here. Nevertheless, it might be the case that both theories can be defended against the dilemma in similar ways. We will come back to this point later.

15. See Stoll (1961: 319), Potter (1990: 56).

16. While the problem of the emptiness of the thesis of universal emptiness raised by the opponent hinges on the misunderstanding of a key concept (taking "empty" to mean "non-existent"), there is a closely associated problem that cannot be resolved so easily. If all things are empty, not just the *assertion* of emptiness must be empty, but emptiness itself as well. However, the properties key Madhyamaka authors ascribe to emptiness (such as not being causally produced, being unchanging, and independent of other things) are just the defining properties of substance. So emptiness seems to be both empty *and* exist substantially, which is a contradiction. For a discussion of various reactions to this problem, see Westerhoff (2009a: 40–46). See also Arnold (2005: 183–192).

17. Boghossian (2006: 53). See also Nagel (1997: 15).

3.1.2. The Sound Analogy [3, 25–28]

3. If you were of the opinion that it is like "do not make a sound," this would not be adequate, for in this case there is the prevention of a future sound by an existing one.

You might be of the opinion that certainly someone who said "you should not make a sound" would himself make a sound, and by this sound there would be the prevention of that other one's sound.

The opponent now suggests an example that Nāgārjuna might want to use to spell out the way in which his thesis of universal emptiness refutes the assertion of substance. If I say to someone "do not utter a word," we can see this in two ways: either as an existent sound preventing a future existent sound, or as an existent sound establishing the non-existence of a sound later on. But unfortunately, neither of the two interpretations is applicable to Nāgārjuna's thesis of universal emptiness seen as refuting the existence of substance or as establishing the non-existence of substance. This is because Nāgārjuna has already asserted that the thesis of universal emptiness is empty, too. We would have to spell out the analogy like this:

In precisely this way the empty statement "all things are empty" dispels the substance of all things.

However, this cannot be right, as the opponent correctly remarks.

Here we say: This is also fails to be accomplished. Why? For in this case the negation of a future sound is brought about by an existent sound. However, for you here the negation of the substance of all things is not brought about by an existent assertion. For according to your opinion the assertion is non-existent and the substance of all things is also non-existent. To this extent, saying that your statement is like "do not make a sound" is an unsuitable assertion.

The analogy does not succeed because whether we see the sound as preventing the existence or as establishing the non-existence of another sound, it is always an *existent* sound which does this. For Nāgārjuna, however, it is an *empty* statement that refutes the existence of substance or establishes the absence of substance. Note that the opponent still takes "empty" to mean "non-existent." But whether or not one makes this erroneous presupposition, the two cases are still structurally different. If the empty thesis of universal emptiness is regarded as *establishing* something, it establishes something of the same ontological quality, namely, the substancelessness of things. If it is seen as *refuting*, it refutes something of the opposite quality, namely, that things have substance. On the other hand, if the existent sound "do not utter a word" *establishes* something, it establishes something of the opposite ontological quality (a non-existent sound later on); if it *prevents* something, it prevents something of the same quality (an existent sound later on). "Do not utter a word" functions differently from "all things are empty"; therefore it cannot be used as an example to illustrate the working of the latter.

REPLY

25. *You did not construct the example "do not make a sound" successfully. That is the prevention of a sound by a sound, but it is clearly not like this in the present case.*

This is not our example. In case someone said "do not make a sound," words are uttered and by them further utterances are prevented. Yet our empty statement does not prevent emptiness in a similar way. Why? There, in the example, sound is dispelled by sound. But it is not like this in the present case. We say "all objects are without substance, and because they are without substance they are empty." Why?

Nāgārjuna agrees with the opponent that the example is not successful for the structural reasons just mentioned. If the statement "do not utter a word" is seen as preventing something, it prevents something of the same ontological status: an existent sound prevents another existent sound from arising in the future. But if the statement "all things are empty" is seen as preventing something, it does not prevent something of the same ontological status. It does not prevent the emptiness of things but establishes it. If it dispels something it does not dispel something of the same kind, as speech dispels speech. As we have seen above, it is not a substantially existent statement that Nāgārjuna uses to dispel the notion of substance, but an empty one.

26. *If substanceless things are refuted by something substanceless, when what is substanceless is abandoned substance would be established.*

When an utterance prevents further utterances, as in the example of "do not make a sound," the example would be appropriate if a substanceless utterance prevented substanceless things. However, in this case the negation of the substance in things is brought about by substanceless speech. In this way, if the negation of the lack of substance in things was brought about by a substanceless speech, things would be endowed with substance because of this very negation of substancelessness. Because of being endowed with substance, they would not be empty. We declared the emptiness of things, not their non-emptiness. The example mentioned is a non-example.

Nāgārjuna continues to point out why the example is unsatisfactory by demonstrating that if it *was* structurally similar to the thesis of universal emptiness, his position would be inconsistent. In the example of "do not utter a word," one thing prevents the existence of another thing of the same ontological status. If "all things are empty" worked in the same way, since we already know that the thesis of universal emptiness is empty, too, we would have the case of an empty thing preventing (or establishing the negation of) other empty things.

But once emptiness is negated its opposite, substance, is established. Since the establishment of substance would contradict the Madhyamaka position, the example cannot be structurally the same as the thesis of universal emptiness.

27. ***The case is rather like an artificial person preventing someone's wrong notion, when that one thinks "this is a woman" about an artificial woman.***

If some man had a wrong conception of an artificial woman empty of substance, thinking "this is really a woman," he might develop desire for her because of that wrong notion. The Blessed One or one of his disciples could then create an artificial man, and by the power of the Blessed One or of his disciple the man's wrong grasping would be prevented. In exactly the same way, the grasping at substance, which is like the artificial woman, is prevented and negated by my empty speech, which is like the artificial man. So this is a suitable example for establishing emptiness, not the one just given.

As a substitute for the unsatisfactory example mentioned by the opponent, Nāgārjuna comes back to the first example of artificially created persons mentioned in verse 23. Suppose a man believes that a woman who exists only in his imagination is real, which leads to all sorts of emotional entanglements. The Buddha could now artificially create another person that cures the man of his illusion. (How the the second person does this can only be guessed at. Perhaps it is a psychiatrist, or perhaps the artificial man runs off with the artificial woman.) Neither the illusion (the artificial woman) nor the cure of the illusion (the artificial man) would have any real existence; nevertheless one would have an effect on the other.

For an analogous example of curing one illusion by another one that involves no illusionists apart from our own mind, consider the following case. Let there be twins of identical height, one of whom wears a horizontally striped dress, the other one a vertically striped one. Because of this the latter will look taller than the former. Now put both of them in a so-called Ames room, a room compressed in one corner so that objects placed there look taller than they are in fact. We can position the twins in such a way that the effects of the striped clothing are offset by the effects of the Ames room, so that the two once more look as if they have the same height.[18]

In the same way in which we do not have to suppose that the erroneous conception of the artificial woman has to be dissolved by a really existent person, but can be dissolved by another artificial person, one non-veridical perception does not necessarily have to be corrected by a veridical one (such as that achieved by having the two twins stand next to a ruler), but can be corrected by a non-veridical perception of a specific type, designed to offset the distortion introduced by the first perception. Both illusion-producer and illusion-remover can be entities of the same kind.

18. For more discussion of this example, see Johnston (1996: 72–82).

It is interesting to note that while the artificial woman is here used by Nāgārjuna as an example of the illusion of substance we perceive in things generally, this example has particular force from the Buddhist perspective, since our ordinary view of women (and men) is similarly lacking in foundation. We think we are surrounded by a collection of more or less stable and autonomous agents and therefore develop all kinds of likes and dislikes toward them. All there is, however, are constantly changing combinations of physical and psychological components that we arrange into person-sized parcels. The teaching on nonself that sets out to refute the ordinary view of persons therefore acts like the Buddha's artificial man that dissolves the wrongly conceived artificial woman.

28. It is rather that the example[19] is of the same nature as what we want to establish,[20] for there is no existence of sound. We do not speak without assenting to the conventional truth.

*The example "do not make a sound" is precisely of the same nature as what we want to establish. Why? Because things are uniformly without substance. There is no substantial existence of that sound because it is dependently arisen. Because there is no substantial existence of it your statement "**3.** [...] **for in this case there is the prevention of a future sound by an existing one**" is refuted.*

We remember that in verse 3 the opponent criticized the example he suggested the Mādhyamika might use in elucidating the working of his thesis of universal emptiness. There the opponent argued that while the Mādhyamika wanted to establish the non-existence of things by a non-existent thesis, in the example "do not make a sound" an *existent* sound was to establish the non-existence of a sound in the future. For this reason, "do not make a sound" could not be used as an example of "all things are emtpy."

Nāgārjuna observes now, however, that the difference between the two cases is only brought out if we assume that the preventing sound and the prevented sound have a different ontological status. But this implies a denial of the thesis of universal emptiness, since for the Mādhyamika *all* things are empty, so that in the final analysis both the preventing sound and the prevented sound have the same ontological status. The opponent therefore helped himself to a denial of the thesis which is under discussion.

19. Nāgārjuna is referring here to the example "Do not make a sound" introduced by the opponent. I follow Bhattacharya (1978: 112, note 1) in assuming that *hetu* is used here in the sense of *dṛṣṭānta*.

20. Nāgārjuna here uses the technical term *sādhyasama*, sometimes translated as *petitio principii* (this term is used again in verse 69). Despite some similarities, the two concepts are not identical, however: *sādhyasama* is not just the assumption of the conclusion to be proved in the premisses. For a discussion of the different uses of the two concepts in Buddhist and non-Buddhist literature, see Bhattacharya (1974), especially 229–230, Matilal (1974), especially 221–222, as well as Bhattacharya et al. (1978: 112–113, note 3).

That everything *is* empty does not imply that the two examples turn out to be analogous in the end:[21] in one case an empty sound *prevents* another empty sound, in the other an empty thesis *establishes* the existence of empty objects. Even if the relata have the same ontological status, the relations employed in the two examples are very different.

We might now think that if everything is empty, the two relations of "preventing" and "establishing" are empty, too, so that the two cases "do not make a sound" and "all things are empty" are in fact analogous: in each case two empty relata are related by an empty relation. While this is true, Nāgārjuna points out that:

We do not speak without assenting to the conventional truth, rejecting the conventional truth when we say "all things are empty." For it is not without having had recourse to the conventional truth that the nature of things can be explained. As it was said:[22]

> *Not having had recourse to the conventional, the absolute is not taught.*
> *Without having approached the absolute, liberation is not reached.*

To this extent all things are empty like my speech, and insubstantiality is established in both ways.

While it is true that in the final analysis everything is empty, and therefore everything is analogous to everything else in this respect, this is not the level at which arguments can proceed. At the level of conventional truth the two relations are distinct, and so the two cases cannot be seen as analogous at this level. It is at this level that all philosophical discussion, including the debate about emptiness, must take place, as Nāgārjuna points out by quoting a verse from his main work, the *Mūlamadhyamakakārikā*. Only at the conventional level are conventionally established systems of shared concepts available, which is a precondition for any philosophical debate. And since the two relations differ at the conventional level, the thesis "all things are empty" cannot be spelled out in terms of "do not make a sound."

It is worth pausing for a moment at this place to appreciate the dialectic of the arguments put forward in this section. At the outset, the opponent puts words into Nāgārjuna's mouth and describes the "do not make a sound" example that he thinks Nāgārjuna might employ to illustrate his theory of emptiness. But he then immediately turns around to say that the example is in fact not adequate. Nāgārjuna agrees with this, argues that the example was not his in the first place, and presents an alternative: the example of the illusory woman. It is

21. As Bhattacharya (1978: 112, note 3) seems to think.
22. *Mūlamadhyamakakārikā* 24:10.

of course slightly curious that both Nāgārjuna and his opponent are equally dismissive of the "do not make a sound" example. The reason that it is included at all, one must suppose, is that is was introduced by someone in defense of the Madhyamaka position. Realizing its problematic nature, Nāgārjuna uses this opportunity to dispose of it.

Up to this point, we have a simple debate about which of two examples is more useful in explaining the theory of emptiness. But in verse 28 things get considerably more interesting. For now Nāgārjuna argues that the initial criticism that the opponent brought forward against the example is not well founded. The reason he is not contradicting his own earlier assertion that the example is in fact a non-example is that the discussion is now conducted at a different level. From the perspective of conventional truth, the two utterances "everything is empty" and "do not make a sound" are sufficiently unlike to make the second useless as an illustration of the first. But this is no longer the case at the absolute level, where everything is equally empty. Of course this helps neither the opponent, who is hardly going to accept the thesis of universal emptiness to salvage his example, nor does it help the unknown first proposer of the example, since the level of absolute truth is not the level at which philosophical debates are conducted. These can only take place on the basis of conventional truth. Verse 28 has turned the comparatively simple debate about which example to use into something more subtle, namely, a question about the level at which philosophical debates happen. Nāgārjuna asserts his commitment to conventional truth as the background against which his arguments, as well as all philosophical debates, are to be understood. Without a firm grounding in the merely transactional reality of conventional truth, the establishment of universal emptiness, which is an ultimate truth, cannot be attained.

There remains one issue in this passage to consider. Nāgārjuna does not tell us what he means by being "established in both ways." The way Bhattacharya renders this passage[23] as well as the accompanying note suggest that he, assuming that Nāgārjuna thinks in the end that "do not make a sound" establishes his thesis of universal emptiness, takes "both ways" to mean "established by 'All things are empty' *and* by 'Do not make a sound.' " As it is not clear to me how "do not make a sound" is supposed to establish universal emptiness, even if all sounds are empty, I do not find this interpretation very convincing.

I suggest we read "both ways" as referring to the two truths just mentioned in the quotation from the *Mūlamadhyamakakārikā*. Emptiness is established by way of conventional truth, since all philosophical debates must happen at this level. It is also established by way of absolute truth, because only at this level

23. 1978: 112.

the conventional is seen as empty of its deceptive appearance of substantiality. At the conventional level, we can *infer* the conventional to be insubstantial, even though it will still appear to us as substantial. Only at the absolute level do we *directly apprehend* the conventional as empty, and only at this level liberation is attained.

3.1.3. The No-thesis View [4, 29]

4. If you thought that the negation's negation is also like this, that would indeed not be correct. Thus your thesis, not mine, is corrupted by the specific characteristic.

You might think "By this very rule the negation's negation fails to be accomplished, and in this context your negating the assertion of the negation of the substance of all things fails to be accomplished."

The opponent now suggests another way in which Nāgārjuna might reply to the charge of argumentational impotence. There are two ways in which we can interpret this suggested reply, one straightforward (and less satisfactory), one somewhat more sophisticated.

According to the straightforward reading, Nāgārjuna might think: "It is true, my thesis of universal emptiness is empty too, and therefore, being non-existent, unable to refute my opponent's assertion of substance. But then, since everything is empty, his refutation of my position is empty, too, thus also non-existent, and therefore argumentationally impotent, too. Therefore the opponent cannot refute me."

Following this interpretation, when the opponent says that Nāgārjuna's thesis "is corrupted by the specific characteristic," he must mean that the thesis of universal emptiness is itself empty and, since "empty" means "non-existent," is itself non-existent. But since Nāgārjuna has already clarified in verse 22 that he does not equate emptiness and non-existence, we may wonder whether something else might not be meant here.

Adopting the second, more subtle reading, which also has the advantage of letting us make better sense of Nāgārjuna's reply in the following verse, it appears that the opponent thinks something else is wrong with Nāgārjuna's claim. The opponent charges Nāgārjuna's thesis with impotence because, being empty, it has to be given a semantics different from the one the opponent favors. Given the Nyāya background of many of the opponent's assertions, it makes sense to attribute to him a realist semantics which assumes that there are mind-independent individuals and properties in the world, that they combine in different ways, and that it is their combinations that make sentences true. The Mādhyamika obviously has problems with such a notion of a ready-made world which does not depend on anything for its existence. And if his theory of universal emptiness makes him reject such a world, he will also have to adopt a different account of what makes sentences true. While the nature of a Madhyamaka-compatible semantics is not addressed much in Nāgārjuna's writings, it seems plausible to suppose that a "worldless" theory based entirely on conventions between speakers would fit the bill. What the precise nature of such a theory would be need not worry us too much here.[24] What is of importance in the context of the present discussion is to understand how someone defending a semantics based on correspondence with a mind-independent world could criticize a convention-based semantics as producing only powerless statements. As Nāgārjuna has to regard his thesis of universal emptiness as empty too, he would have to supply it with such a convention-based semantics. But then, the opponent will object, his thesis will never get out of the domain of conventions and connect up with the real world, in the way the statements of the opponent, which are to be supplied with a realist semantics, do. For the opponent, Nāgārjuna's thesis compares to his philosophical statements like money made playing Monopoly to money made in the real estate market: the first is perfectly functional in the context of the game but, unlike the second, cannot be used to buy anything outside the game. Monopoly money can only buy Monopoly houses, but real money can buy not just real houses, but all sorts of other things as well. This interpretation of what the opponent means by his charge of argumentational impotence is considerably more interesting than the one based on a misunderstanding of "empty" as "non-existent."

Here we say: This is also not correct. Why? Since the specific characteristic of the thesis applies to your thesis, not to mine. You say "all things are empty," I do not. The initial position is not mine. In this context, your statement that while it is like this, the negation's negation fails to be accomplished is not tenable.

Once again, the opponent's answer can be read in two ways, depending on how we interpret the reply he has just suggested to Nāgārjuna.

According to the first reading, the reply turns out to be hopelessly circular. For it is only once we accept the thesis of universal emptiness (together with an assumption that Nāgārjuna does not share, namely, that emptiness implies non-existence and hence argumentational impotence) that we can regard the opponent's attempted refutation as similarly powerless as our own statements. Then we could claim that even though the thesis of universal emptiness—if true—cannot refute the opponent, the opponent cannot refute it either, since his counterargument is equally empty and therefore equally powerless. But, of course, the opponent does not accept the thesis of universal emptiness. Its truth or falsity is what the debate is about, so we can hardly defend it by an argument that assumes its truth.

24. For some ideas see Westerhoff 2010.

On the second interpretation, however, the criticism the opponent attributes to Nāgārjuna becomes somewhat more powerful. For if the opponent sets out to refute Nāgārjuna's thesis of universal emptiness, he either takes it as having significance outside of Nāgārjuna's system of conventions and therefore worthy of refutation, or he regards the statement he wants to defend (the negation of Nāgārjuna's thesis) to have merely conventional significance, too, since merely adding the word "not" does not switch the interpretation of the statement from a conventional to a substantial one.

What the opponent might respond here is that there are two ways of negating Nāgārjuna's thesis, one of which is presupposition-preserving and one which is not.[25] Consider, for example, the statement "the number 2 is red." We can negate it in a way that preserves the presupposition that the number 2 has some color ("the number two is not red but green") or we can negate it by rejecting this presupposition ("the number is not red, nor any other color"). In the same way, the opponent can deny the thesis of universal emptiness without accepting the presuppositions about the right kind of semantics the thesis makes.

REPLY

29. If I had any thesis, that fault would apply to me. But I do not have any thesis, so there is indeed no fault for me.

This is certainly the most famous and also one of the most puzzling verses in the entire text. It it quoted frequently in the Buddhist commentarial literature,[26] though the uses to which it is put are very diverse.[27] Although tracing the variant interpretations of this verse across nearly two millenia of Buddhist writing would be fascinating and rewarding, this cannot be our aim in the present context. We want to understand how the verse fits into the overall structure of argument presented in the *Vigrahavyāvartanī*.

If I had any thesis, the earlier fault you mentioned would apply to me, because the mark of my thesis has been affected. But I do not have any thesis. To that extent, while all things are empty, completely pacified, and by nature free from substance,[28]

25. The distinction between these two kinds of negation, called *paryudāsa-pratiṣedha* and *prasajya-pratiṣedha*, is used in the later Madhyamaka literature, though Nāgārjuna does not make any direct reference to it. For more on these, see Ruegg (2000: 117), (2002: note 6, 19–24), Westerhoff (2006).

26. For example, in Candrakīrti's Prasannapadā (La Vallée Poussin 1903–1913: 16:7–8); Tsong kha pa Blo bzang grags pa (1985: 677, 687), Tsong kha pa Blo bzang grags pa (2000–2004: III:230, 241); mKhas grub dGe legs dpal bzang (1983: 295), Cabezón (1992: 257), Cabezón and Lobsang Dargyay (2007: 106–109). See also dGe 'dun chos 'phel (No date: 22–28), Lopez (2005: 64–70). A good overview of its uses in the Indo-Tibetan tradition is in Ruegg (1983). Further references to western commentarial literature on this verse are given in Lopez (1994: 162, note 5). See also Napper (1989: 116–122).

27. Westerhoff (2009b), Lopez (1994; 2005: 151–159).

28. The term Nāgārjuna uses here is *prakṛti-vivikta*. In his commentary on the *Aṣṭasāhasrikāprajñāpāramitā* (Wogihara 1932–1935: 443), Haribhadra glosses the terms *prakṛti-viviktatva* as *svabhāva-śūnyatva*, that is, emptiness of substance. See also Warder (1980:351). Bhattacharya et al. (1978: 113, note 2) reads the compound

from where could a thesis come? From where could something affecting the character of my thesis come? In this context your statement "there is precisely that fault for you, because the mark of your thesis has been affected" is not tenable.

In order to understand this verse, it is first of all essential to realize that Nāgārjuna does not make the obviously false claim that he asserts no theses whatsoever.[29] After all, there are the *Mūlamadhyamakakārikā*, the *Vigrahavyāvartanī*, and so forth, all of which are filled with philosophical theses and thereby contradict this way of understanding Nāgārjuna's verse. What Nāgārjuna wants to say here is that he does not have any thesis *of a particular kind*,[30] that is, that among the theses one should assert there is none which exists substantially, none which is to be interpreted according to the familiar realist semantics just described. If there were any statements which had to be supplied with a realist semantics, while others are only given a conventionalist semantics, then it is true that the "earlier fault" would apply. The second kind of statement would be powerless to refute the first kind.

Consider the following example. Some people believe that there are rules which are grounded in something distinct from a set of human conventions. They might think that some rules (the substantial rules) are reflections of norms existing out there in the world. For example, one might assume that our penal code contains a prohibition against murder because it is a fact about the moral world that murder is wrong. Even realists about moral norms, however, do not think that *all* rules are grounded like that. There is no fact out there determining which side of the road is the right one for driving on, and it is not the case that either the English or the French have a defective understanding of the Rules of the Road instantiated in some abstract realm. We are dealing here with a purely conventional rule settled by a system of human agreements. Now it is evident that in a world in which there are substantial and conventional rules, the conventional rules can never overrule the substantial ones. When there is a conflict between the two, it is always the conventional rule which has to give way—because it is only grounded in human practices, but not in the way the world is.

The same happens when statements come in two flavors: one, those put forward by the opponent, deriving their meaning and truth-value from the world

differently and takes it to mean "having a nature, a 'universal and absolute Reality' which is isolated from its appearances." I do not share this interpretation.

29. For more on the use of the term "thesis" (*pratijñā*) in Madhyamaka literature, see Ruegg (1983: 213–215); (1986: 232–235).

30. The insertion of such modifiers is often necessary when interpreting Madhyamaka texts. As a hermeneutic technique it is much employed in the dGe lugs commentarial tradition beginning with Tsong *kha pa*, who justifies it with a quote from the *Laṅkāvatārasūtra* (Tsong kha pa Blo bzang grags pa 2000–2004: 3:188). It is, however, not without its critics even in the Tibetan tradition.

out there; the others, Nāgārjuna's, deriving these from their location in a system of conventions. In this case, a convention-based statement would not be able to refute a substantial one.

However, when asserting that he has no thesis, Nāgārjuna rejects this two-flavor theory of statements. Once the nature of conventions employed has been seen through and is thereby "completely pacified," it becomes evident that there are no statements which have to be supplied with a realist semantics. As all statements Nāgārjuna asserts (and therefore all statements the philosopher in general should assert) are to be supplied with the same convention-based semantics, the charge of powerlessness does not apply. The mark of Nāgārjuna's thesis, namely its emptiness, which requires it to be spelled out in terms of a convention-based semantics, does not render it impotent because of the claim that some theses have to be supplied with another kind of semantics, since the very existence of such a realist semantics is ruled out by the Madhyamaka theory of emptiness.

A similar strategy suggests itself to the global relativist in reply to the dilemma mentioned on page 54. It is obviously unsatisfactory to embrace the first horn of this dilemma, arguing that the thesis of global relativism holds absolutely, in the same way in which it would have not been very convincing for the Madhyamaka to assert that all things are empty, apart from those which are not, such as the thesis of universal emptiness. The objective is then to argue that embracing the second horn, that is, claiming that the thesis of global relativism itself is only relatively true, does not undermine its philosophical force. For it is of course true that if there are truths made true by the world, then truths made true only by a theory appear insubstantial in comparison. But the global relativist, like Nāgārjuna, will want to deny that such a two-flavor picture obtains, and has to offer arguments to this effect. If this is successful, that is, if he has shown that all truths are relative, then stating that a particular one, such as that of global relativism, is merely relative will not detract from its status. The question then becomes why this relative truth, rather than another one, should be adopted. This question, however, is one we have to address for any statement we want to adopt in the relativist framework. It does not pose a specific problem for the thesis of global relativism.

3.2. Epistemology [5–6, 30–51]

3.2.1. Establishing the Epistemic Instruments [5–6, 30–33]

The following two verses mark the beginning of a long section concerned with epistemology. Nāgārjuna responds to the criticism voiced here in the following twenty-two verses; this amounts to nearly half of all the responses he gives in the text.

5. If you deny objects after having apprehended them through perception, that perception by which the objects are perceived does not exist.

In the first four verses, the opponent's main worry was the status of the thesis of universal emptiness to the extent to which it applied to itself, as it is empty like everything else. His present concern is how it fits with accounts of the theory of knowledge. What epistemological story can we tell in order to explain how we arrive at the thesis of universal emptiness?

If, having apprehended all things by perception, one then negates the things by saying "all things are empty," that negation fails to be accomplished. Why? Because it is included among all things, perception, the epistemic instrument, is also empty. Who conceives of objects is empty as well. To this extent there is no thing apprehended by perception, the epistemic instrument. The negation of something unperceived fails to be established. In that context, the statement "all things are empty" fails to be accomplished.

The following discussion is based on the four epistemic instruments assumed in the Nyāya theory of knowledge: perception, inference, testimony, and likeness.[31] Perception is considered first. In order to come up with any theory of objects (whether it is a scientific theory or a philosophical one like those presently under discussion), we first have to have knowledge of these objects. Then we can come up with an account of how they work, their inner nature, and so forth. The obvious and most common way to acquire such knowledge is by sensory perception. But the Madhyamaka theory short-circuits this epistemological process. The opponent argues that the Madhyamaka first helps himself to substantially existing epistemic instruments in order to establish his theory of universal emptiness and then turns around, saying that there are no substantially existing epistemic instruments. If everything is empty, an epistemic instrument like perception is empty, too. And the opponent still has worries about how empty things can fulfill a function. If these are justified, then the theory of emptiness cannot get off the ground, for there are no epistemic objects in the first place for it to be a theory of. The negation contained in the statement of universal emptiness has to operate on something, and if there is nothing to negate, there will be no negation either.

Note that this "self-stultification objection"[32] could be raised even if the opponent were not to believe that that "empty" meant "non-existent." For Nāgārjuna has to assert that the epistemic instruments are not instruments by their nature, so that ultimately there are no epistemic instruments. Thus ultimately the truth of emptiness could not be established, even if it obtained, since some epistemic instruments would be necessary for its establishment.

31. See Chatterjee (1978).
32. Siderits (2003: 140).

The same difficulties apply to the epistemic agent, who is supposed to acquire the knowledge of the object by means of perception in order to build a theory around it. As this agent is empty, too, it is similarly unclear how he can play any role in the epistemic process.

In the contemporary discussion of science, we sometimes find the assertion that common sense leads to physics, and that physics shows that common sense is mistaken. In a similar way, we can understand the opponent here as saying that Nāgārjuna's philosophical theory (or *any* theory, for that matter) needs the epistemic instruments to construct it. But then Nāgārjuna undermines the foundation of his own theory, the opponent argues, since it denies the existence (or at least the ultimate reality) of the epistemic instruments that established it in the first place.

The opponent continues:

You might think, "The rejection of all things is brought about after having apprehended them either by inference, testimony, or likeness."

Of course, perception is not the only way in which we can acquire knowledge of objects. We can also draw inferences about an object that is not there to be perceived, can be informed about it by a trustworthy witness, or find out about it because it is similar to another thing we do know. So perhaps we can form a notion of an object by one of these means and then have the thesis of universal emptiness apply to these objects.

Here we say:

6. Inference, testimony, and likeness are refuted by perception, as well as the objects to be established by inference, testimony, and example.

"Objects to be exablished by example" is used here to refer to what is apprehended by the fourth epistemic instrument, likeness.

Inference, testimony, and likeness are refuted by perception, the epistemic instrument. For as perception, the epistemic instrument, is empty because of the emptiness of all things, in the same way inference, likeness, and testimony are also empty because of the emptiness of all things. The objects to be established by inference and the objects to be established by testimony and likeness are also empty because of the emptiness of all things. Who apprehends things by inference, likeness, and testimony is also empty. Therefore there is no apprehending of things, and for things which are not apprehended the negation of substance fails to be established. In that context, the statement "all things are empty" is not tenable.

What the opponent wants to say here is not that perception refutes the other three epistemic instruments, but that the difficulty identified for perception extends to any of the other epistemic instruments. Verse 6 expands the point made in verse 5 to the remaining three epistemic instruments other than perception, as well as to the epistemic objects and the epistemic agent. All of these are all empty too, and for the opponent this casts doubt on their functionality. If "empty" means "non-existent," Nāgārjuna faces the difficulty how non-existent instruments can accomplish anything, or how a non-existent object could be known by a non-existent epistemic agent. But even if the opponent does not adopt this reading, it seems as if the best these empty epistemic instruments could provide are empty epistemic objects, known by a cognizer who is empty, too. But none of this, the opponent argues, provides a sufficiently stable epistemic basis for constructing any theory, including the theory of universal emptiness. If ultimately there are no epistemic instruments, no agent who employs them, and no epistemic objects, then ultimately emptiness is unknowable.

REPLY

30. If I perceived anything by means of perception, I would affirm or deny. But because that does not exist, there is no criticism applicable to me.

"That" here refers to the presupposition of substantially existent epistemic instruments.

If I apprehended any object by the causes of knowledge, by perception, inference, likeness, or authority, or by any particular one of the four epistemic instruments, I would indeed affirm or deny. But because I do not propound any object I do not affirm or deny.

In this context, your criticism is this: "If you deny any objects after having apprehended them by one of the epistemic instruments, such as perception and so forth, while these epistemic instruments do not exist there are also no objects accessed by these epistemic instruments." But this criticism does not apply to me.

It is interesting to note that in this verse Nāgārjuna does not respond to the criticism put forward by the opponent in verses 5 and 6 with the obvious reply that "empty" does not mean "lack of causal efficiency." We recall that in the two preceding verses the opponent has voiced the doubt that empty epistemic instruments can fulfill any function, such as making known an epistemic object, based on the (mistaken) understanding that the emptiness of the epistemic instruments implies that these epistemic instruments do not exist. This point was already addressed by Nāgārjuna in verse 22, where he noted that an object's emptiness does not preclude it from performing a function.

Apart from the fact that he already pointed this out earlier in the text, the main reason why Nāgārjuna does not just answer the opponent by noting that empty epistemic instruments can nevertheless be efficient is to forestall an objection analogous to the one described in my comments on verse 29. If there are empty as well as non-empty epistemic instruments, the non-empty instruments, the instruments which are intrinsically means of acquiring knowledge, will have an epistemologically more prestigious status. This is why Nāgārjuna sets out to demonstrate that the very notion of substantial epistemic instruments is incoherent.

This is why he rejects the idea that he would affirm or deny any objects as existing substantially, after having apprehended them by one of the epistemic instruments *as understood by the opponent*. Nāgārjuna does not accept the substantial existence of epistemic instruments, while the opponent does.

He therefore starts to launch a counterattack against the opponent's theory of knowledge. According to the opponent, there are objects out there in the world about which we form beliefs by perception, inference, testimony, and likeness. On the basis of the information supplied by these epistemic instruments, the intrinsic nature of which is to supply us with knowledge of the world around us, we then make positive or negative judgments about the epistemic objects apprehended. Nāgārjuna will use the following verses to demonstrate that this epistemological picture is deeply unsatisfactory. His aim is to replace it with an epistemological theory that incorporates empty epistemic instruments; apprehending things by these is compatible with instruments and objects of knowledge being equally insubstantial.

31. If, according to you, objects of some kind are established by the epistemic instruments, you have to indicate how according to you the epistemic instruments are established in turn.

If you think that epistemic objects of some kind are established through the epistemic instruments, just as a measuring instrument establishes what is to be measured, then where does the establishment of the four epistemic instruments, perception, inference, likeness, and testimony, come from? Because if the epistemic instruments were established by something that was not an epistemic instrument, the thesis that "the objects are established through the epistemic instruments" is refuted.

Suppose we find out about the properties of some object by applying an epistemic instrument to it, as we find out about the length of something by measuring it with a ruler, or about its weight by putting it on a pair of scales. Mirroring the opponent's earlier worry about the emptiness of the thesis of universal emptiness in verse 1, Nāgārjuna now queries the establishment of the instruments that are supposed to establish the epistemic objects. Whatever establishes them must be an epistemic instrument, too, since the epistemic instruments are part of the world, and the opponent claims that our epistemic access to the world is made possible by epistemic instruments.[33] Nāgārjuna will come back to this point soon.

33. *Nyāyasūtra* 4.2.29 states that "things are cognized by the epistemic instruments" (*pramāṇataś ca cārthapratipatteḥ*). Uḍḍyotakara expands on this: "What exists and in what manner it exists, as also what does

32a. If the epistemic instruments were established by other epistemic instruments, there would be an infinite regress.

If you thought that the epistemic objects are established by the epistemic instruments, and that the epistemic instruments are established by other epistemic instruments, the absurd consequence of an infinite regress follows. What is the problem with the absurd consequence of an infinite regress?

32b. Neither the beginning, the middle, or the end are established there.

There is the absurd consequence of an infinite regress, the beginning is not established. Why? Because those epistemic instruments are established by other epistemic instruments, and so in turn for these other epistemic instruments. Because there is no beginning, where would middle and end come from? To this extent your statement "the epistemic instruments are established by other epistemic instruments" is not adequate.

Nāgārjuna notes here that founding our knowledge of objects on the epistemic instruments is not satisfactory if the epistemic instruments themselves require justification.[34] How do we know that perception is a reliable way of accessing the world? According to the opponent, this would mean that there is an epistemic instrument out there that has a particular property, namely, accurately representing the world. But *this* fact has to be established by some epistemic instruments, too. Once we accept that, nothing will keep us from repeating this move as often as we want.[35] We therefore never reach the epistemic rock bottom that we thought the epistemic instruments could provide.

Assume you employ visual perception to find out whether a particular peg will fit in a particular hole. Visual inspection of peg and hole shows that the sizes fit and leads to successful practice in fitting one inside the other. But to justify visual perception as an epistemic instrument because it leads to successful practice, we need a further perception in order to determine that we actually were successful. In this case we need a further epistemic instrument, and so on.

Can this regress be stopped? One thing we could say, and this is indeed the response given by the Naiyāyika, is that while such a regress is possible in theory, in practice we never demand justification beyond one or two steps.[36] If we doubt whether there really is a dagger floating in front of us, we might

not exist, and in what manner it does not exist, all this is ascertained through what we cognize by the epistemic instruments," (*yadasti yathā ca yannāsti yathā ca tat sarvaṃ pramāṇata upalabdhyā siddhyatīti*). (1916: 520).

34. It is interesting to note that the Bhāṭṭa Mīmāṃsakas use this very regress argument in order to establish that the epistemic instruments must possess intrinsic validity (*svataḥ prāmāṇya*). See Sāstrī (1926: verses 49–51, pages 90–91), Arnold (2005: 69–70).

35. Siderits (2003: 140) interprets Nāgārjuna as employing a destructive trilemma to argue against the existence of epistemic instruments by showing that these involve either an infinite regress, circularity (see verse 46), or arbitrariness (see page 92 above).

36. *Nyāyasūtra* 2.1.8–20.

go and have our eyes checked, but we would then not challenge our belief in the truth of what the ophtalmologist tells us, or our belief in whatever corroborates his assertions. After a few justificatory iterations, our doubts tend to disappear.[37]

The difficulty with this position is, of course, that our actual epistemic practice could just be wrong. Even if we think that we do not require any more justification after one or two steps, this is in itself nothing but a reflection of our own psychological demands, but does not imply anything about the justification of the epistemic instruments.[38]

33. "These are established without the epistemic instruments"—your position is abandoned. There is an inequality to be explained, and you should state the special reason.

Then if you think "these epistemic instruments are established without epistemic instruments, but the objects to be known are established by the epistemic instruments," your position "objects are established by epistemic instruments" is abandoned. There is an inequality to be explained, since some objects are established by epistemic instruments, and some are not. You should state the special reason why some objects are established by epistemic instruments and some are not. As this is not specified, your supposition is not adequate.

The obvious reply to this charge of an infinite regress is to point out that the epistemic instruments do not need further epistemic instruments in turn to be established. Why not? The opponent does not say. One thing he could say, though, is that the epistemic instruments have no explicit proof because they need none—they are just instruments establishing the nature of their objects. They are not epistemic objects that need to be established. This in effect amounts to rejecting any theory of the epistemic instruments. As such, this reply would not be very attractive to the Naiyāyika, since he does have a fully worked-out theory of the epistemic instruments. Moreover, it seems to be difficult to assert that the epistemic instruments are distinct from epistemic objects and thus do not need to be established themselves in the absence of any theory of such instruments.[39]

But independent of *why* the opponent claims that the epistemic instruments do not need to be established by other instruments, Nāgārjuna objects that such a move would imply that the opponent can no longer hold that *everything* knowable is known through epistemic instruments, since this does not include the

37. Siderits (1980: 331).

38. Of course, one might respond that justification is necessarily always "piecemeal and local." But this leads to a kind of coherentism that is difficult to bring into accord with the Nyāya views of epistemic instruments. See Siderits (2003: 141).

39. Siderits (1980: 312).

epistemic instruments. This thesis is something the Naiyāyika would be very reluctant to give up.

Next we see Nāgārjuna use the same structure of argument against the opponent that was used against himself earlier in verse 2. If the opponent wants to argue that the epistemic instruments are in some way exceptional, he has to state the special property epistemic instruments have so that they need not be known by epistemic instruments themselves.

At this point the opponent objects: "It is the very epistemic instruments which prove themselves as well as others. As it is said:

> *As fire illuminates itself as well as others, so the epistemic instruments prove themselves and others.*[40]

As fire illuminates both itself and others, the epistemic instruments illuminate both themselves and others."

The opponent now comes up with an idea that allows him to hold on to the idea that *everything* is known by epistemic instruments and could also solve both the *regress problem* and that of the *inequality to be explained* that is, something that tells us why the epistemic instruments constitute a special class of objects which are not in turn known by *other* epistemic instruments. He suggests that the epistemic instruments establish themselves. Instead of telling us in detail how this is supposed to work (how does perception itself tell me perception is an epistemic instrument?), the opponent gives us an illustrative example.

A fire illuminates objects that were previously hidden in the dark and makes them known to us in this way. But we do not need a second fire to illuminate the fire, and then a third to see the second illuminating fire, and so on. While a fire stands in the "illuminates" relation to things around it, it also stands in this relation to itself. So, the opponent argues, as there is no infinite regress in the case of the fire there should be none for the epistemic instruments, either.

To illustrate the same point with a more modern example: sometimes we need to open files on our computer that have been compressed, that is, specially encoded to use less storage space. We then run a decompression program on the file in order to read it. The decompression program itself, however, usually comes to us in compressed format. If we now needed another decompression program to unpack it, we would be well on our way to an infinite regress, as we would never have a decompressed program to start the whole chain. The answer to this problem is simple, of course: the compressed decompression program is stored in a self-extracting file—it is able to decompress itself.

40. The source of this quotation is unclear. Even though it is very close to the statement made in the *Nyāyasūtra* 2.1.19 up to now it has been impossible to locate it in any extant Nyāya work. See Meuthrath (1999:8, note 24; 14).

The example of the self-illuminating fire solves the problem of the *inequality to be explained* by denying that any such inequality exists. It is not the case that "some objects are established by epistemic instruments, and some are not," since in fact neither the objects nor the epistemic instruments can be known without the epistemic instruments: the epistemic objects need the instruments to know them, and the instruments need themselves to be known.

There is an interesting similarity between the verses 32–33 and verses 17–19 from the second *adhyāya*, first *āhnika* of the *Nyāyasūtra*.[41]

17. *If the epistemic instruments are established by epistemic instruments, it follows as a consequence that there is an establishment by other epistemic instruments.*
18. *Or, if this is given up, the establishment of epistemic objects would be like the establishment of the epistemic instruments.*
19. *No, the establishment of epistemic instruments is like the light of a lamp.*

Fleshing out these rather terse statements a bit, the argument seems to be something like the following: If the epistemic instruments establish other epistemic instruments there is an infinite regress, because for the establishment of each instrument we need a new instrument, and then a new instrument for establishing that, and so on. Alternatively, if the idea of such a regress was abandoned, the other option open to us was that the epistemic instruments are established without requiring epistemic instruments. But then we might wonder why the epistemic objects needed the instruments for their establishment, since there now turn out to be things (namely, the epistemic instruments) that can be known without requiring the use of epistemic instruments. Unless we have some account of the specific characteristic of the epistemic instruments that could account for this, it is not clear why the epistemic objects could not also be established without the instruments in the same way. As a response attempting to show that these difficulties can be solved, the comparison with the light of the lamp is then introduced.

When the argument is expanded in this way, the parallels with Nāgārjuna's verses seem obvious. Both texts note the same difficulties for the idea that epistemic instruments establish other epistemic instruments: an *infinite regress* and an *inequality to be explained*.[42] Both texts then suggest the comparison with a self-illuminating source of light. Nevertheless, whether this apparent similarity means that Nāgārjuna and the *Nyāyasūtra* actually have the same argument in

41. *Nyāyasūtra* 2.1.17–19.

42. Unlike the *Nyāyasūtra*, Nāgārjuna uses the technical terms *anavasthā* and *vaiṣamikatva* (the latter apparently meaning the same as *vaiṣamyadoṣa*) to describe these.

mind and understand the example of the self-illuminating object in the same way is something contemporary scholars do not agree on.[43]

To this we reply:

3.2.2. The Fire Analogy [34–39]

34. This is a mistaken suggestion. For fire does not illuminate itself, as not perceiving it is not similar to the sight of a pot in the dark.

It is clearly a mistake to suggest that the epistemic instruments prove themselves and prove others, because fire does not illuminate itself. For if at first the pot in the dark, which is not illuminated by fire, is not perceived, it is perceived at a later time, being illuminated by fire. If there was first an unilluminated fire in the dark, which would be illuminated at a later time, then fire would illuminate itself. However, it is not like this. So far this assumption is not adequate.

This is the first of six verses in which Nāgārjuna points out the difficulties of understanding the establishment of the epistemic instruments along the lines of the illumination by a fire. When trying to make sense of these, it is useful to take into account two parallel passages from Nāgārjuna's works where he discusses the same example: *Mūlamadhyamakakārikā* 7:8–12 and *Vaidalyaprakaraṇa* 6–11.[44]

In the present verse, Nāgārjuna begins by addressing the assumption that a fire illuminates itself. What we mean by "*x* illuminates *y*" is that first of all *y* exists in darkness, where it can be perceived by sensory faculties other than sight. We can touch a pot in the dark, hear its sound if we bump into it, and so forth. The object is then subsequently touched by light, and thereby becomes visible to us. If, however, *x* and *y* are identical, then *the very same object* must exist first in darkness and then be illuminated. But in a dark room there is no fire yet. None of our other sensory faculties can perceive anything like the hotness or the sound of fire when its illumination is absent. The fire's illuminating power and its existence come into being at the same time. For this reason, assuming

43. Oberhammer (1963: 66) and Oetke (1991: 33–34) argue that they do not, Yamaguchi (1929: 68–70), Bhattacharya (1977: 271), Bronkhorst (1985: 111), and Meuthrath (1999: 11–15) that they do.

Another question arising in this context is whether the similarities allow us to infer anything about the relative date of the two texts. Was the passage in the *Nyāyasūtra* composed after the *Vigrahavyāvartanī*, and perhaps even as an explicit reaction to Nāgārjuna's arguments, as argued by Ruben (1928: 24) and Oberhammer (1963), or is it the other way round (Bhattacharya 1977)? Or do both derive from a common source of arguments and comparisons present in the Indian philosophical debate before either text was composed (Oetke 1991: 54)? As we are presently mainly interested in the philosophical content, I will not pursue questions of chronology. The interested reader will find an excellent survey of the issue in Meuthrath (1999).

44. In the passage from the *Vaidalyaprakaraṇa* the example is clearly used for the same purposes as it is here. In the *Mūlamadhyamakakārikā*, the context is somewhat different: here Nāgārjuna uses the example of the self-illuminating fire when discussing the question whether birth can bring forth itself.

that fire illuminates itself does not cohere with our use of the concept of illumination.

35. ***If, according to your assertion, fire illuminates itself like others, is it not also the case that fire consumes itself?***

If, according to your assertion, as fire illuminates itself in the very same way as it illuminates other things, is it not also the case that it consumes itself in the very same way in which it consumes other things? However, it is not like this. In this context, the statement "fire illuminates itself in the same way in which it illuminates others" is not tenable.

Nāgārjuna now here comes up with a second absurd consequence of assuming that fire can illuminate itself. Not only would there have to be an invisible fire in the dark, the fire that consumes the firewood would also have to consume itself. Note that Nāgārjuna does not rely on the incorrect principle that if one quality of an object acts on the object itself, any other quality will do so too. That a barber shaves himself does not imply that he also cuts the hair on his own head, as these two actions are completely independent of one another. But the consumption of firewood and the illumination are the very same process seen from two different perspectives. And a process that is reflexive under one description has to be so under any other one.[45]

In this case, self-illumination would imply self-consumption. However, the fire does not consume itself, because what we mean by "x consumes y" is that there is a certain quantity of y at the outset, and during some process in which x and y are both causally involved y becomes gradually less. But this entails that "fire consumes fire" is not a satisfactory description of what happens when a fire burns. It is not always the case that a conflagration starts with a certain amount of fire (however this is to be quantified), which gradually decreases as the fire keeps burning. Frequently there will be just a small flame in the beginning that increases in size and, having reached its maximal extension, dies down. This can easily be explained by conceptualizing fire as consuming fuel, but not by conceptualizing it as consuming itself.[46]

45. In fact this maxim is subject to some qualifications. Cutting myself in the finger is a process that is reflexive under one description, but presumably not under another one phrased entirely in terms of molecules bumping against each other. What we would want to say is that if two descriptions of a process involve the same individual ("fire," in our case) and coreferential relation-terms with different senses ("illuminates" and "consumes"), then the process is reflexive under all descriptions if and only if it is reflexive under any.

46. *Pace* Bhattacharya et al. (1978: 117–118, note 1) it is not necessary to interpret the argument here as based on the "anti-reflexivity principle" (*svātmani-kriyā-virodha*) found in Indian philosophical literature; see Siderits (2003: 32, note a). Rather than appealing to this principle (which is backed up by its own illustrative examples, such as the sword which cannot cut itself) and thereby concluding that fire cannot be self-consuming, it is sufficient to make the far simpler point that self-consumption does not allow us to make good sense of our observations of fires.

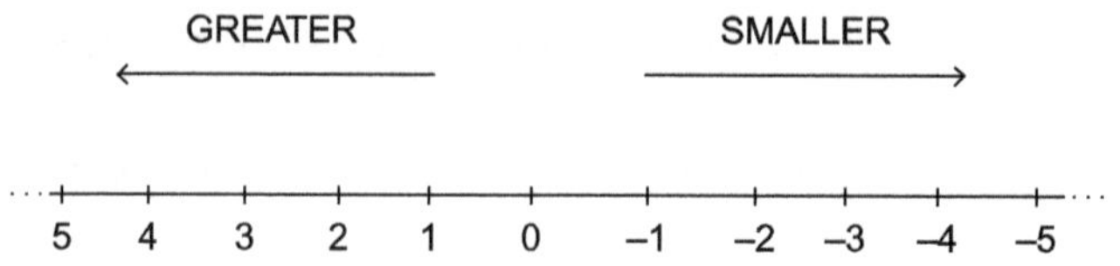

FIGURE 1.

*36. **If, according to your assertion, fire illuminates both itself and others, darkness will conceal both itself and others, in the same way as fire.***

If you thought fire illuminates both itself and others, would it not now be the case that the opposite thing, darkness, would also conceal both itself and others? But this is not observed. In this context your statement "fire illuminates both itself and others" is not tenable.

This point seems to have been important for Nāgārjuna, as he makes it in two other places, in *Mūlamadhyamakakārikā* 7:12 and *Vaidalyaprakaraṇa* 11. The argument relies on the assumption that if a relation *R* relates an object to itself, the "opposite" of *R* must also relate the "opposite" of the object to itself. Whether this assumption is plausible is not easy to evaluate, mainly because it is difficult to come up with a sufficiently clear general conception of the "opposite" of an object.

The model in figure 1 could be used as an illustration. Let our objects be the positive integers and let the "opposite" of an object be the corresponding negative integer (that is, the opposite of 5 is −5).[47] Take the relation "*x* is greater than a predecessor of *y*,"[48] which, for example, applies to the numbers 5 and 4, but also to each positive integer itself, since each positive integer is greater than its own predecessors. This relation does not hold for the negative integers, however, since, for example, −5 is smaller than its predecessor −4. Since we regard the negative integers as the "opposites" of the positives the *opposite* of this relation should also relate all the negative integers to themselves. We construct the "opposite" of "*x* is greater than a predecessor of *x*" by replacing the notion "greater than" by its opposite[49] "smaller than." It is now easy to see that this relation does indeed relate all the negative integers to themselves, since each is smaller than its own predecessors.

This model provides us with an example of a case where the fact that a relation relates an object to itself implies that the "opposite" of the relation must

47. Technically speaking, the negative number structure is the dual of the positive number structure.

48. Imagine the integers arranged on a line with zero in the middle, the positive integers to the left and the negative integers to the right. An integer *a* is a predecessor of *b* if *a* is closer to zero than *b*, if it is further away than *b* it is a successor.

49. Technically speaking: "its dual."

also relate the "opposite" of the object to itself. If we suppose that this holds in general, and also assume that "darkness" and "*x* conceals *y*" are the opposites of "light" and "*x* illuminates *y*," it is apparent that light cannot be self-illuminating. We do perceive darkness, for example, after blowing out a candle in a windowless room, but if darkness really concealed itself we should not be able to do so.

David Burton claims that the argument expressed in this verse

> relies on the assumption that darkness is in fact the opposite substance to light. But the Naiyāyikas maintain—sensibly, I think—that whereas light (*tejas*) is a substance (*dravya*), darkness (*tamas*) is an absence (*abhāva*).... Thus Nāgārjuna's argument fails:... darkness is not the opposing substance to light. Rather it is a mere absence of light.[50]

This criticism appears to encounter both historical and systematic difficulties. First, whether darkness should be included among the substances was a matter of debate.[51] Second I do not see any systematic reasons why the argument "substance *a* has property *P*, therefore the absence (*abhāva*) of *a* has the opposite of the property *P*" is substantially weaker than the argument "substance *a* has property *P*, therefore substance *b*, which is the opposite of *a*, has the opposite of the property of *P*," especially if the absence of something, which may well be regarded as its "opposite," is regarded as a category in its own right. It is therefore far from evident whether a Nyāya-Vaiśeṣika account might be able to get around the unwanted consequence that darkness conceals itself. But even if this could be done, it would not imply that "Nāgārjuna's argument fails": in order to show this we would also have to demonstrate that this Nyāya-Vaiśeṣika account was the position Nāgārjuna was trying to refute. Given that the textual evidence in the *Vigrahavyāvartanī* only allows us general conjectures about the views of the respective opponents, it becomes difficult to see how such a demonstration could be accomplished.

37. There is no darkness in the blazing, nor in something else in which there is blazing. How does it do the illuminating, as illumination is the destruction of the dark?

Here there is no darkness in the fire and there is also no darkness where the fire is. Illumination is precisely the prevention of darkness. As far as darkness is not in the fire, and no darkness is where there is fire, which darkness does the fire prevent, and by the prevention of what does it illuminate both itself and others?

Again, there are two passages closely similar to the point made here, in *Vaidalyaprakaraṇa* 10 and *Mūlamadhyamakakārikā* 7:9b. In the present verse Nāgārjuna points out that darkness is not somewhere concealed inside of the

50. 1999: 168.

51. Burton refers to the *Vaiśeṣikasūtra* 5.2.19–20 (Chakrabarty 2003: 80), but see Halbfass (1992: 73).

flame, nor present in something of which the flame is part (such as the causal field consisting of fuel, oxygen, and so forth). But this is what we have to assume if fire is regarded as self-illuminating. For when fire illuminates an object, it simultaneously acts on the darkness obscuring the object and eliminates it. But if "*x* illuminates *y*" and "*x* eliminates the darkness obscuring *y*" are the very same act, the self-illumination of the fire also means that it eliminates the darkness obscuring it, a darkness which is either present within the fire or in its surroundings. Once again this is hardly in accordance with our observations of fire. We do not observe any darkness within the fire, nor is a fire which is about to be lit enveloped in darkness that it dispels when starting to burn.

At this point the opponent objects: "As far as there is no darkness in the fire in this way, and as there is no darkness where there is fire, why does fire not illuminate both itself and others? For precisely the arising fire prevents darkness. As far as there is no darkness in the fire, and no darkness where there is fire, so far precisely the arising fire illuminates both itself and others."

The opponent agrees that it is not satisfactory to assume that darkness is contained in the fire or in its surroundings after the fire has originated. This, however, does not necessarily imply that the self-illumination of fire is impossible. For it could be the case that at the very moment at which the fire is about to originate, fire and darkness coexist. Fire and darkness are both present for one moment, then the fire begins to act on the darkness in order to remove it. When we say that fire illuminates itself and spell this out as "fire itself removes the darkness obscuring it," we refer to this moment of coexistence of fire and darkness when illumination is just about to begin, not to any darkness contained in a blazing fire or its surroundings.

To this we reply:

38. "Precisely the arising fire illuminates"—this position is wrong. For that very arising fire does not connect with darkness.

The assertion that "precisely this arising fire illuminates itself and others" is not established. Why? For that very arising fire does not connect with darkness. Because of the lack of connection it does not destroy darkness, and because darkness is not prevented, there is no illumination.

But the difficulty with assuming a momentary coexistence of darkness and the originating fire is that we then have trouble explaining how the fire ever manages to remove darkness at all. If fire and darkness can coexist during one instant, what keeps them from coexisting for another instant? Or, put the other way around, what makes fire causally efficacious in removing darkness in the second instant, but not in the first?[52] The opponent would certainly need to

52. *Mūlamadhyamakakārikā* 7:10.

provide some explanation why the lack of causal connection between fire and darkness during the moment of origination is not perpetuated.

39. ***But if an unconnected fire were to prevent darkness, the fire present here would prevent the darkness in all worlds.***

If you think "an unconnected fire also prevents darkness," would it not be the case then that the fire present here right now will similarly prevent that unconnected darkness located in all worlds? But this is not what we observe. So far your asserting that "precisely the unconnected fire prevents darkness" is not tenable.

The opponent might now object that a particular connection between fire and darkness such as would be required in the second moment of existence of the fire is not necessary. Why he thinks so is not made explicit. But we might fill in the opponent's argument here by looking at parallel passages in Nāgārjuna's other works. In verse 8 of the *Vaidalyaprakaraṇa*, the opponent raises the possibility that two things could interact without any contact between them. He supports this by an astrological example. In ancient India the planets were thought to exercise an influence on human beings, though they were obviously not in any kind of spatial contact with them. Perhaps fire and darkness could interact in a similar way without requiring a specific connection.

But this response has the unwelcome consequence that we now have a hard time explaining why lighting a candle in my room does not remove the darkness in the room next door, but only the darkness immediately surrounding it.[53] Why does the mysterious "action at a distance" not similarly act on darkness somewhere else, so that a light here can illuminate darkness far away? Usually lack of spatial connection is a good explanation for why one thing cannot act on another one: I cannot cut myself with the knife in the next room because it is not spatially connected with me.[54] So if illumination can remove darkness without a connection there is still a difference between the unconnected darkness in my room that the candle can remove and the equally unconnected darkness in the other room that it cannot remove. A "no connection" view of illumination would have to explain this difference.

It is interesting to note that Nāgārjuna himself says in *Vaidalyaprakaraṇa* 7 that no connection between illumination and darkness is even possible. This is because we should not think of illumination and darkness as two kinds of objects that somehow have to connect to interact with one another, as, for example, water has to connect with salt in order to dissolve it. Illumination and darkness are opposed entities; where one is, the other is not. One can be understood as the absence of the other: illumination is the absence of

53. *Mūlamadhyamakakārikā* 7:11, *Vaidalyaprakaraṇa* 8.

54. Nāgārjuna uses this example in *Vaidalyaprakaraṇa* 7.

darkness, and darkness is the absence of illumination.[55] It therefore does not make sense to require some kind of connection between illumination and darkness, as they are not the kinds of objects that can meet eye-to-eye at the ontological level, since the existence of one necessitates the non-existence of the other.

This reply is immune from the objection just made, that an unconnected illumination would illuminate all darkness whatsoever. For if illumination and darkness are understood as mutual absences, rather than as independent objects, it is clear why the darkness in the room next door is not illuminated by the candle in here. As a given illumination only covers a specific finite area, the absence of darkness it brings about only extends to the very same area. The illumination of the candle does not connect with the darkness in this room because there is no independent thing called darkness it could connect with. It is also true that it does not connect with the darkness next door, but all we mean by this is that the illumination or absence of darkness produced only covers a certain amount of space, and that this does not include the space in the room next door.

Although it thus makes sense to say that light and darkness do not come into contact with each other, this particular view is hardly one the opponent would want to adopt. This is because if illumination and darkness cannot coexist (since they are mutual absences), the opponent's assumption made after verse 37 that they exist simultaneously at the moment of the fire's origination cannot be maintained. For this reason, the opponent cannot maintain that illumination and darkness interact in the way he envisages them to do while maintaining that there is no connection between the two.

This verse ends the specific consideration of the analogy of the self-illuminating fire. After setting out to establish that we cannot argue for the self-establishment of the epistemic instruments by analogy with the self-illumination of fire (because fire does not illuminate itself), Nāgārjuna now points out another unsatisfactory consequence should we maintain their self-establishment nevertheless.

3.2.3. The Epistemic Instruments as Self-established [40–41]

40. If the epistemic instruments are self-established, the epistemic objects will be independent of the establishment of the epistemic instruments for you, for self-establishment is not dependent on anything else.

55. *Svavṛtti* on *Vaidalyaprakaraṇa* 9, *Mūlamadhyamakakārikā* 7:9a. The conceptualization of darkness as an absence was fairly common among the Indian philosophical schools. See Jhalakīkar (1996: s. v. *tamaḥ*, 319–321), Tola and Dragonetti (1995: note 6, 186).

If you think "the epistemic instruments are self-established like fire," the establishment of the epistemic instruments will also be independent of the objects to be known. Why? Because what is self-established does not depend on anything else. Moreover, what is dependent is not self-established.

If the epistemic instruments establish their own veridicality, they do not require any other entities to do this for them; in particular, they do not need to be established by the epistemic objects.

At this point the opponent objects, "If the epistemic instruments do not depend on the objects to be known, what is the problem?"

While it is clear that an epistemic instrument such as visual perception establishes the existence of objects seen, why should the objects seen be required to establish perception? There does not seem to be any problem with attempting to establish the epistemic instruments without referring to the objects known.

To this we reply:

41. *If for you the establishment of the epistemic instruments is independent of the objects to be known, then those will not be the epistemic instruments of anything.*

If the establishment of the epistemic instruments is independent of the objects to be known, those epistemic instruments would not be the epistemic instruments of anything. This is the problem. Moreover, the epistemic instruments are epistemic instruments of something, therefore in this case the epistemic instruments are precisely not independent of the objects to be known.

Assume that the epistemic instruments were self-established, that is, they had some property analogous to the supposed self-illumination of fire. We can imagine all sorts of epistemic practices, some of which we usually regard as routes to knowledge (such as perception and inference) and others that we do not regard as such (tea-leaf reading, answering a question by tossing a coin). The idea is now that the respectable epistemic practices, that is, the epistemic instruments, establish their own veracity, while the more dubious methods do not do so. But without looking at the objects known, how do we know that self-establishment really is the mark of an epistemic instrument? After all, the only thing we know is that there is a very diverse collection of epistemic practices, some of which have a specific property analogous to the supposed self-illumination by fire. But how do we know that this property does not rather mark the epistemic practices that are *not* epistemic instruments? We can only do so by referring to the objects known. Only by finding out that vision reliably tells us whether an apple is red or green, thereby allowing us to successfully distinguish apples, but that closing our eyes and tossing a coin does not, can we determine that vision, which is supposedly self-established, is an epistemic instrument while coin-tossing is not. Once we have established that the analogue of the supposed self-illumination indeed gives us knowledge of the nature of the epistemic objects and correlates with successful interaction with them, can we regard this property as an indication of an epistemic instrument. But if this is the case, then the epistemic instruments are not purely self-established, since ascribing the status "epistemic instruments" to them requires reference to the epistemic objects at a crucial point. We therefore have to reject the kind of epistemic foundationalism which assumes that the epistemic instruments are intrinsically such instruments, and replace it by a contextualism asserting that what counts as epistemic justification is always dependent on factors extrinsic to the instruments, such as the set of objects among which the inquiry is conducted.[56]

We can compare the situation with the following case. Suppose we are given five bottles with different liquids and are asked to find out which is the best glue. Assume further that we assess the quality of the glue in terms of the fracture resistance of the bonded structure that is the result of the gluing. The important point now is that no amount of intrinsic information about the contents of the bottles (such as the ratio of the different ingredients, or even the molecular structure of the liquids) allows us to answer this question, since no liquid is intrinsically a glue or not; it is only a glue *in relation to objects glued*. Without taking the different materials to be glued into consideration, we cannot rate the quality of the glues, for it might be the case that even the most inactive of the liquids proves to be a glue of incredible strength when applied to some outlandish material.[57] As we have to refer to the objects glued in order to rate the different liquids (indeed even to identify them as glues), we have to refer to the epistemic objects in order identify something as an epistemic instrument.

3.2.4. Epistemic Instruments and Their Objects [42–48]

42. Moreover, if one thought "the establishment of those is dependent," then what is the problem here? There would be the establishment of the established, because what is not established does not depend on another thing.

Moreover, if one also thought "the establishment of the epistemic instruments is dependent on the epistemic objects" in this case there is the establishment of the established fourfold epistemic instruments. Why? Since there is no dependence for an unestablished object. An unestablished Devadatta does not depend on any object. The

56. See Siderits (2003: 146).

57. A short story by the German author Kurt Kusenberg describes an inventor who develops a glue that does not glue anything. Because of its pleasant scent it is mainly used as a perfume. The inventor therefore produces a material (called "nihilit") that has no other purpose but to be glued by the sweet-smelling liquid and turns out to be useless for anything else.

establishment of the already established is not sensible; there is no making of what one has already made.

The opponent might now bite the bullet and claim that the establishment of the epistemic instruments will indeed require reference to, and thus depend on, the epistemic objects. The motivation for this may be the intuition that the objects known are somehow prior to the instruments that bring about knowledge of them. But in this case he is in the curious position of using knowledge of the objects in order to establish which epistemic practices are epistemic instruments. Such knowledge, however, can only come through the epistemic instruments, which therefore already have to be established. Establishing them again via the epistemic objects is superfluous.[58]

43. If the epistemic instruments are established dependent on the epistemic objects in every context, then the establishment of the epistemic objects is precisely not dependent on the epistemic instruments.

If the epistemic instruments are established dependent on the epistemic objects, then in this case the epistemic objects are not established dependent on the epistemic instruments. Why? For the thing to be established does not establish the instrument for establishing. And the epistemic instruments are said to be the instruments for establishing the epistemic objects.

Furthermore, if the epistemic objects are required in order to establish the epistemic instruments, we get into difficulties with the usual assumption that it is the epistemic instruments which establish the objects. We find out about the color of the apple by using the instrument of visual perception, but can we then also use the color of the apple to establish something about visual perception?

Reversing a relation of establishment does not necessarily lead to problems. We can use a measuring jug to establish some volume of liquid is a liter, and we can also use the liter in order to establish the accuracy of the measuring jug.[59] If, however, we are looking for some sort of foundation of the accuracy of the measuring jug, we would better not test it by using its own measurements as a benchmark. Similarly, if we want to establish the role of certain epistemic practices as epistemic instruments, we cannot then ground our knowledge on whatever results the epistemic practices themselves produce.[60]

44. And if the establishment of the epistemic object is precisely independent of the epistemic instruments, what is achieved for you by establishing the epistemic instruments? Their purpose is already established.

58. Compare *Mūlamadhyamakakārikā* 10:9a.

59. Similarly a weight can be used to measure other objects or it can be weighed itself to test its accuracy. See *Nyāyasūtra* 2.2.16.

60. Compare *Mūlamadhyamakakārikā* 10:10–11.

If you think "the establishment of the epistemic objects is precisely independent of the epistemic instruments," what is achieved for you in this context by seeking the establishment of the epistemic instruments? Why? The epistemic objects, which are the purpose why one looks for the epistemic instruments, are established even without the epistemic instruments. What is to be achieved by the epistemic instruments in this case?

Nāgārjuna here considers the inverse of the assumption made in verse 41: the establishment of the epistemic objects is independent of the epistemic instruments. But if *this* is what the opponent thinks, it is unclear what the purpose of the entire debate is. If the objects known are already established in some way, why do we worry about the status of some epistemic practices that have no impact on our knowledge of the world in any case? The only reason we worry about the epistemic instruments is because we want to use them as a means of getting at the epistemic objects. If they do not have to fulfill this role they become theoretically superfluous.

45. But then for you the establishment of the epistemic instruments is precisely dependent on the epistemic objects. This being so, epistemic instruments and objects are in fact reversed for you.

Moreover, if you think "the epistemic instruments are precisely dependent on the objects to be known, so there should not be the problem mentioned earlier,"[61] *it follows that, epistemic instruments and objects being reversed for you, the epistemic instruments become epistemic objects because they are brought about by the epistemic objects, and the epistemic objects become epistemic instruments because they bring about the epistemic instruments.*

This verse takes up the position set out in verses 42 and 43, that is, that the epistemic instruments are established in dependence on their objects. There it was noted that this would entail that epistemic instruments which already have to be in place to generate knowledge of objects are established once more, and would furthermore reverse the ordinary view that it is the *objects* which are established, not the instruments. As Nāgārjuna points out now, if we regard the epistemic objects as what is established and the instruments as the establisher, and also assume that the epistemic instruments are established by the objects, this turns the instruments into epistemic objects while the epistemic objects, which are to establish the instruments, turn into instruments themselves, as they now fulfill the function of the establisher.

46. Furthermore, if for you the establishment of the epistemic objects is by the epistemic instruments and the establishment of the epistemic instruments by the epistemic objects, neither is established for you.

61. In verse 41.

Furthermore, if you think "the establishment of the epistemic objects is by the epistemic instruments because of the dependence on the epistemic instruments, and the establishment of the epistemic instruments is by the epistemic objects because of the dependence on the epistemic objects," neither is established for you. Why?

The opponent might consider the fact that the epistemic instruments and objects can be reversed in the way described in the last verse as not much of a problem. For if the two establish each other mutually, this is exactly what we would expect: the epistemic instruments are instruments *qua* establishers of the objects, and objects *qua* established by the instruments; the objects are objects *qua* established by the instruments and instruments *qua* establishers of the objects. As Nāgārjuna is going to point out, however, this does not give us a way of establishing either of them.

47. Because if these epistemic objects are established by precisely these epistemic instruments, and if these are to be established by the epistemic objects, how will they establish?

Because if these epistemic objects are established by the epistemic instruments, and if the epistemic instruments are to be established by precisely these epistemic objects, should we not ask how the unestablished epistemic objects will establish something, as the epistemic objects are unestablished, since their cause is unestablished?

If we use the epistemic instruments to ground our knowledge of objects in the familiar way, but then have to ground the instruments in terms of these very objects, we have not grounded anything at all, but have just gone around in a circle.

48. And if these epistemic instruments are established by precisely these epistemic objects, and if these are to be established by the epistemic instruments, how will they establish?

And if these epistemic instruments are established by the epistemic objects, and if the epistemic objects are to be established by precisely these epistemic instruments, should we not ask how the unestablished epistemic instruments will establish something, as the epistemic instruments are unestablished, since their cause is unestablished?

If, on the other hand, we use reference to the objects in order to establish the epistemic instruments, as suggested in verse 42, but then need the instruments in order to establish the objects, we have not succeeded in constructing a foundation either, but have just gone around in a circle in the reverse order.

There are two different argumentative aims we can attribute to Nāgārjuna in noting the mutual dependence of epistemic instruments and objects. First, it can be seen as a *reply to the Naiyāyika's self-stultification objection*. As such, it is not in itself meant to refute the Nyāya attempt to determine reliable epistemic instruments. Nāgārjuna is rather making the point that if we accept the thesis of universal emptiness, there can be no epistemic instruments independent of human conceptualization. It is then unsatisfactory to argue, as the Naiyāyika does, that the absence of epistemic instruments, which are instruments substantially, that is, instruments the intrinsic nature of which makes them reliable means of cognition, means that emptiness could not be established at all. The proponent of the thesis of universal emptiness who denies the independence of any objects from conceptualization need not first establish reliable epistemic instruments in order to use these to gain access to epistemic objects, as the Naiyāyika demands. Given the Madhyamaka's central claim, there would be no point in following the Nyāya epistemological project.

Second, one might also think that Nāgārjuna does something more substantial by claiming that epistemic instruments and objects are mutually dependent. This is not just intended as a reply to the Naiyāyika, but is rather the basis for an *epistemological argument for the thesis of universal emptiness*. What could this argument be?

We should first note that the most we could hope to achieve by the kind of mutual establishment of the instruments and objects of knowledge described in the present and in the preceding verse is an epistemological system based on coherence. We begin with some pre-theoretical beliefs about objects that appear trustworthy and use them to test assumptions about epistemic instruments. Then we use these instruments to refine our beliefs about objects. After that, we employ these objects in order to justify further instruments that produce knowledge of yet more objects, and so on. Like people finding some planks on the seashore, we build a boat to cross the ocean, and once we are afloat we find new planks in the sea that we use to expand and repair our boat. Our boat does not depend essentially on the first planks we used; similarly, our theory does not depend essentially on our first unquestioned assumptions. Both may be replaced and discarded at some point in the process without the whole system ceasing to be functional.

But since our boat does not essentially depend on the first planks we used, it could have been the case that we had ended up with a different boat, which would have been able to keep us afloat just as well. It is similarly possible that we might end up with a different mutually coherent set of instruments and beliefs about objects than the one we in fact acquired. But if this is the case, then we can never be certain that we have got it right: developing a reflective equilibrium in which epistemic instruments and objects are carefully balanced never gives us a way of connecting our epistemic instruments with the nature of things, as the Nyāya realist requires. In the beginning, our set of epistemic instruments and objects will only have an initial plausibility conditional on our first set of unjustified and unjustifiable assumptions. Further down the road, when these assumptions may no longer be in play, the plausibility of the set depends solely on the mutual coherence of its members. But neither of these provides the kind of foundation the realist requires. Unjustified assumptions cannot provide it, and considerations of coherence only appeal to logical relations between cognitions. They do not provide us with the knowledge of any objects these cognitions may be cognitions of.[62] We can never be certain whether our epistemic instruments are true to the nature of the objects they provide us with information about. The whole notion of a reliable epistemic instrument ceases to make sense, and the distinction between ontology and epistemology that the critic of the thesis of universal emptiness has to defend seems to vanish.[63]

The difficulty with this second, philosophically more substantial, interpretation of Nāgārjuna's assertion of the mutual dependence of epistemic instruments and objects are the internalist and verificationist assumptions it makes. An epistemic internalist will claim that to have a justified true belief one must have knowledge of this justification; it is not sufficient just to *be* justified. This means that the fact that I cannot know what reliable epistemic instruments there are implies that there are no such instruments. The verificationist will assert that if I could not possibly find out whether some statement was true (such as the statement that something is an epistemic instrument), the statement is meaningless. The epistemic externalist, on the other hand, draws a line between *there being* epistemic instruments and *us knowing* that there are any, or what they are. The former can obtain without the latter, and in particular we can investigate the epistemic instruments in the way we can investigate any other epistemic objects, and if the results of applying the instruments both to the objects as well as to themselves yield coherent results (as they do), we can regard this as providing probabilistic evidence for the claim that the instruments, indeed "get it right."[64]

The Naiyāyika is neither an epistemic internalist nor a verificationist. As such, it is implausible to read Nāgārjuna's point in a way that only makes sense if it ascribes to his opponent assumptions that he does not share, a move the Madhyamaka's argumentative framework does not allow. Mark Siderits makes the noteworthy point that there is in fact an interesting argument the Madhyamaka can make against the Nyāya epistemology which does not rely on ascribing internalist and verificationist assumptions to it.[65] This argument is not mentioned explicitly by Nāgārjuna, but can be easily extrapolated from his works, and finds better textual support in Āryadeva's writings.[66] The basic idea is that

62. Siderits (1980: 317–318).
63. Siderits (1988).
64. See (2000: 227–229; 2003: 141–142, 147).
65. Siderits (2000: 229–230).
66. See, for example, his *Catuśataka* 13:12 (Dhondhup 2007: 20–21), Rinchen (1994: 257).

if causation is a conceptual construct, as the Mādhyamika analysis attempts to show,[67] something that is an epistemic instrument, a cognitive conduit the reliability of which is assessed using causal vocabulary, must similarly be a cognitive construct. It cannot be a substantially existent epistemic instrument which possesses reliability as part of its intrinsic nature. Epistemic instruments only become such within a specific context of human conventions. Interpreted in this way, the Mādhyamika criticism of Nyāya epistemology and the realism it entails can be understood as being based on externalist assumptions that the Naiyāyika shares.

3.2.5. The Father–Son Analogy [49–50]

49. If the son is to be produced by the father and if the father is to be produced by this very son, you have to say which produces which in this context.

If someone said "the son is to be produced by the father, and this father is to be produced by this very son," in this context you have to say now "which is to be produced by which." Just like this, you say "these very epistemic objects are to be established by the epistemic instruments, and, what is more, the epistemic instruments are to be established by those very objects." In this case now, which ones are to be established by which ones for you?

Nāgārjuna now considers an example that suggests another way of understanding the mutual dependence of epistemic instruments and objects mentioned in the three preceding verses 46–48. Suppose someone argued that the son is to be produced by the father (because if the father did not exist, the son would not exist, either), but that the father is also produced by the son (since if the son did not exist, that man would not be a father). According to this understanding, they mutually depend on each other, though by different dependence relations: the son depends on the father for his *existence*, while the father depends on the son for his *classification as a father*—even as a childless man he would still exist; he would just not be a father.[68] Unlike in the account discussed in the three preceding verses, the existential dependence does not go both ways. One direction is only notional dependence, that is, it is only dependence for description or classification.

We could make the same point for epistemic instruments and objects. It can be represented in the diagram in figure 2. As indicated on the left-hand side of the second box (A), it is possible to say that the instruments depend for their existence on the objects. If there were no objects whatsoever, the epistemic

67. See Siderits 2004.
68. Nāgārjuna mentions the same example in *Śūnyatāsaptati* 13.

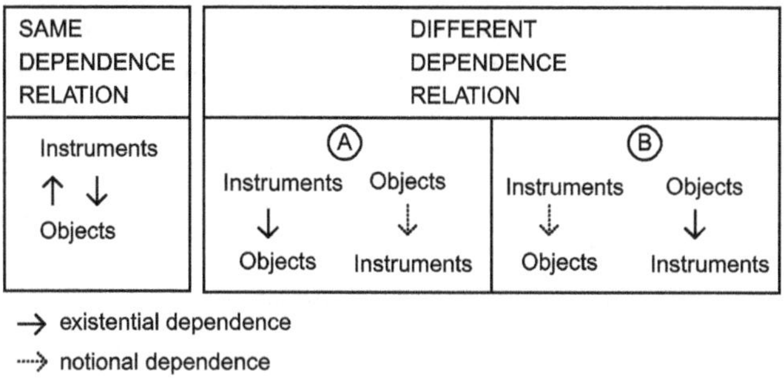

FIGURE 2.

instruments could not be implemented by any biological structures. If there were objects but they were all unknowable, nothing could exist that would make these objects known.

The objects also depend on the instruments for being called "objects," for in a world without observers there would still be things, but we could no longer call them "epistemic objects."

The inverse (B), that is, claiming that the objects depend for their existence on the instruments while the instruments depend on the objects for being called "instruments," is only sensible if we could envisage a world in which there are epistemic instruments (though they would not be called that), but no objects, ruling out that the instruments could ever know themselves (since they would be objects in this case). How to make sense of fundamentally relational phenomena like perception in the absence of one of the relata (namely, the object perceived) is, however, entirely unclear. This inverse reading is therefore hardly satisfactory.

Nāgārjuna then observes that as long as we do not specify which dependence relation we have in mind, we cannot say whether the father is prior to the son or vice versa, since we have to ask, "Prior in respect to what: its existence or its name?" In a similar way, it is unclear what is to ground what: the instruments the objects or the objects the instruments?

*50. **In this context, you should say which is the father and which is the son. Since both have the characteristic of father and son, this case is not clear to us.***

Of the two just mentioned, father and son, which one is the father and which one is the son? Both have the characteristic of the father because they bring about something, and both have the characteristic of the son since they are brought about by something. In this case it is unclear to us which of the two is the father and which is the son. It is the very same with your epistemic instruments and objects: which of them are epistemic instruments and which are epistemic objects? For both are epistemic instruments because they establish something, and both are epistemic objects because they are to be established by something. In this case it is unclear to us which of these are epistemic instruments and which are epistemic objects.

Even if we specify the different dependence relations involved and thereby make it clear what depends on what (as demanded in the preceding verse), the problem remains that if the epistemic instruments and objects are mutually dependent, it cannot be the case that one is intrinsically an establisher and one intrinsically something to be established. While we might think that an epistemic instrument is an establisher by nature, it is also an established (since it depends existentially on the objects). And while the objects are established by the instruments and depend on them for being called "epistemic objects," they are also their establishers, since without objects there would be no instruments. The opponent wants to argue that the epistemic instruments and objects are establishers and established by nature; however, this claim turns out to be inconsistent with assuming that they are mutually dependent.[69]

3.2.6. Summary [51]

51. The epistemic instruments are not self-established, nor are are they mutually established or established by other epistemic instruments, nor are they established by the epistemic objects or established without reason.

Nāgārjuna uses this concluding stanza of his discussion of epistemology in order to summarize the possible ways in which the epistemic instruments could be established. Two of them, self-establishment and establishment by the epistemic objects, have already been discussed in detail. The remaining possibilities have not been considered so far; nevertheless, in the end all of them are rejected as deficient.

Perception is not self-established by that very perception, or inference by that very inference, or likeness by that very likeness, or testimony by that very testimony.

The self-establishment of the epistemic instruments was brought up in the commentary on verse 33 by the example of the self-illumination of fire. Verses 34–41 give the reason why this position is rejected.

Perception is not established by something else, by inference, likeness, or testimony; inference by perception, likeness, or testimony; likeness by perception, inference, or testimony; testimony by perception, inference, or likeness.

Alternatively, one might think that if the epistemic instruments cannot establish themselves they can mutually support each other, without requiring anything they are in turn based on, much as the elements of a self-supporting vault

69. The tension between these two claims is discussed in the *Nyāyasūtra* 15–16. See Jha (1984: 2:628–645).

keep each other in place without the need for a central pillar supporting the whole.

Suppose I find out by perception that I have a fifty-pound note in my wallet. But if I somehow thought my senses were deceiving me, I could call in other epistemic instruments as support. The receipt confirming that I just withdrew fifty pounds from the bank and the fact that I did not have any time in between to spend the money allow me to *infer* that I still heave the money on me. Alternatively, I could argue that the perception of the note in my wallet is sufficiently *like* my other perceptions, such as that of my two hands, which I have reasons to believe to be veridical. Finally I could rely on the *testimony* of other customers at the bank who saw me taking out the money.

Since we can tell a similar story for each of the remaining three epistemic instruments, we could argue that they are established by mutual coherence, that is, by the fact that the information supplied by one of them is usually confirmed by the other three. Such an argument, however, will only let us move in a circle, since we never go beyond the supposed set of epistemic instruments but merely shift the burden of legitimization from one subset to another.

It is also not the case that each one—perception, inference, likeness, or testimony—is established by another perception, inference, likeness, or testimony.

Alternatively, we could assume that epistemic instruments are supported by other epistemic instruments *of the same kind*. This argument can either go backward or forward in time. On the one hand, I can say that I trust the visual perception of the fifty-pound note now because I trusted other perceptions yesterday. And I trusted these because I trusted still others on the day before. Or I can confirm the perception of the banknote five minutes ago by one two minutes ago, this by one sixty seconds ago, and so on. By doing either of these, we are obviously facing a regress having to supply ever new items of perception further away in the past or more and more close to the present.[70]

Nāgārjuna now leaves it to the reader to infer that neither the circularity nor the regress resulting from these attempts at establishing the epistemic instruments will be acceptable to the Naiyāyika opponent who proposes them. As a

70. As Nāgārjuna already observed in verse 32. Matilal (1986: 56) is correct in saying that sometimes there might be "a very pragmatic solution" to such a regress. I trust my visual perception of the banknote today since it is pretty much like my visual perception yesterday, and I trusted this earlier perception. We could then leave it at that because the question concerning the validity of yesterday's visual perception may not have arisen. Something might have prompted me to suspect *today* that I was hallucinating banknotes, but not yesterday. So only today's visual perception needs support, not yesterday's, thereby stopping the regress.

Unfortunately this does not present us with a general way of seeing how an instance of an epistemic instrument could be established by more instances of the same kind. Since we may not always be so lucky that questions of the validity of the supporting instance of the epistemic instruments do not arise, this pragmatic solution cannot be applied in all cases.

realist he has to argue that at some point his epistemic instruments hook up with the objects in order to present accurate knowledge of them. But all he is presenting here is more epistemic instruments: either the task of establishing is moved around between different subsets of epistemic instruments, or it is handed down an infinite chain of particular instances of one epistemic instrument. But a thousand naked men do not make a single dressed one; likewise, a similarly large set of connections between epistemic instruments does not result in a single connection between an epistemic instrument and an epistemic object.

They are also not established by the epistemic objects either collectively or individually, included in their own field or in another. The epistemic instruments are also not established without a reason.

As Nāgārjuna pointed out in verses 42, 43, and 45, the epistemic instruments cannot be established in dependence on individual epistemic objects or on all of them together. This is the case whether or not the object in question is specifically assessed by a particular epistemic instrument. The cup we perceive in front of us has no greater power to establish perception (the means by which we perceive it) as an epistemic instrument than the fire on a distant mountain, which is an epistemic object that can only be accessed by a different epistemic instrument, namely inference. Finally, it is not satisfactory to hold that the epistemic instruments are established without a reason, claiming that it is a brute fact that certain means, such as perception, inference, and so forth, are epistemic instruments while others, such as tea-leaf reading and coin tossing, are not. For a realist like the Naiyāyika, there must be some reason why some means are able to connect with the nature of things and thereby provide us with knowledge, while others are not.

They are also not established by the collection of causes mentioned earlier, 20 or 30 or 40 or 26.

Neither the content nor the meaning of this list of numbers is quite clear. The Tibetan translation gives it as "20, 30, 40, 36," the Chinese[71] as "20, 30, or 40, 50, 60, 20, 30, 40, 50; or 60." Bhattacharya suggests reading *śatavimśati* = "hundred times twenty" instead of *ṣaṭviṃśati* = 26.[72] This would have the advantage of giving a numerical progression which increases in size. We could then read Nāgārjuna simply as saying that the epistemic instruments are not established by any set of causes, regardless of its size. This makes sense, as the causes would in turn be either epistemic instruments or epistemic objects,

71. Tucci (1929: 54).
72. Bhattacharya (1978: 124–125, note 3).

thereby reducing this to a position already discussed. The remaining worry with this interpretation is that there is no earlier place at which Nāgārjuna mentions collections of causes of the epistemic instruments having the respective number of members. We could try to avoid this problem by following Tucci's suggestion, when he claims that the numbers do not refer to the cardinality of the collections of causes but to verses of the *Vigrahavyāvartanī*.[73] But apart from the fact that the verses in question do not mention collections of causes either, this then leads to the problem (which Tucci seems to be aware of) that *Vigrahavyāvartanī* 20, which is given in all three versions of the numerical list, is not concerned with the epistemic instruments at all.[74]

Your earlier statement, "because the things to be known are to be understood by the epistemic instruments, these things to be known exist as well as those epistemic instruments by which the things to be known are accessed" is not tenable.

Nāgārjuna now concludes his survey of the different possible ways of establishing the epistemic instruments by noting that the opponent has not succeeded in showing that a satisfactory epistemology entails that the epistemic instruments as well as their objects cannot be empty. In fact, the theory presented by the opponent leads to a variety of difficulties described above. We realize in particular that the position of the mutual establishment of the epistemic instruments and objects which the opponent is forced to adopt in the end will not allow him to assume that epistemic instruments and objects are instruments and objects by their intrinsic nature. He cannot claim that the epistemic instruments are essentially establishers, while the epistemic objects are essentially the established. But if they lack such intrinsic properties, they are empty. Their emptiness, moreover, does not restrict their functionality. They are still able to play the key roles in epistemology usually ascribed to them.

For the Madhyamaka, the fact that ultimately there are no epistemic instruments and epistemic objects does not mean that emptiness cannot be known. For there are still epistemic instruments that are instruments in a certain context of inquiry, even though they are no such instruments substantially, by their intrinsic nature. In other words, we can still distinguish between epistemic procedures that are and those that are not means for apprehending epistemic objects at the conventional level. This also throws an interesting light on the variety of different arguments for emptiness we find in the Madhyamaka literature. This is not a manifestation of the fact that their authors found none of them completely convincing (for if they did, why come up with more?), but rather results

73. 1929: 40.

74. Tucci claims that "there is the difficulty that the 20th *kārikā* contains the last argument of the *pūrvapakṣa*." It seems to me that the problem is not that the opponent is speaking in verse 20 but that it deals with a completely different topic.

from the Madhyamaka view of epistemic justification. The absence of substantially existent epistemic instruments entails that there can be no argument for emptiness which works in all contexts.[75] Different philosophical methodologies will lead to different formulations of realism and thereby to different argumentational strategies the Madhyamaka would use to argue against them. That there is no one argument which works at all times and against all opponents does not mean that the thesis of universal emptiness cannot be established at all, but only that different contexts necessitate the use of different sets of conventionally established epistemic instruments.

3.3. Intrinsically Good Things [7–8, 52–56]

7. People who know the state of things think that auspicious phenomena have an auspicious substance. This distinction also holds for the other things.

The opponent now sets out to attack Nāgārjuna's theory of universal emptiness by providing an example (which he assumes Nāgārjuna will accept) of some objects that have their nature substantially, and that are representative of other things that also have their natures substantially. The example he uses are the mental events that the Buddhists regard as auspicious or meritorious. As such, the opponent argues, they should be intrinsically meritorious and therefore not empty.

In this context, people who know the state of things have the 119 auspicious things in mind.

Neither the contents of the following list nor the purpose it is to serve is quite clear. This is partly due to the corruptions in the Sanskrit text and the omissions in the Tibetan and Chinese translations (neither of which actually lists 119 items)[76] and partly due to the fact that until now it has been impossible to trace similar enumerations elsewhere.[77] There is a substantial overlap with lists like that of the fifty-two mental formations[78] and of the eleven mental qualities that are "auspicious by nature"[79] given in the Asaṅga's *Abhidharmasamuccaya*, or that of the ten states "which accompany all good minds" that Vasubandhu

75. Siderits (2000: 228; 2003: 147).

76. This is not the only case of a problem with numerical lists in Nāgārjuna's works. Compare Hahn (1982).

77. Comparisons of all three lists and attempts to reconstruct the original version can be found in Tucci (1929: 26–32) and Johnston (1938). The translation of the list given below is meant as a rough guide only; as the terms are all without context and often have a variety of meanings, it is difficult to determine in some cases which one was intended—*caveat lector*. For a more precise account, a comparison with the above two compilations is recommended.

78. Rahula and Boin-Webb (2000: 8–18).

79. *kuśalacaitta, dge ba'i sems byung bcu gcig*, Rahula and Boin-Webb (2000: 45).

mentions in the *Abhidharmakośabhāṣya*.[80] Unfortunately, these similarities do not help us to clarify the most puzzling aspects of this enumeration of 119 auspicious things. Particularly confusing is the fact that a multitude of items in the list are not auspicious at all, for example, items 40 (being not conducive to liberation), 59 (lack of devotion), 74 (anguish), and so forth. Johnston argues that the "true explanation" of this is that the first eighty-one members of the list are only partly auspicious, while the rest of the enumeration (beginning with the phrase "moreover, there is") lists wholly auspicious mental events.[81] This appears to conflict with, for example, items 12 (wisdom) and 13 (equanimity), which seem to be wholly auspicious, and item 46 (utter torment) which is presumably not auspicious at all. Similarly items 113 (lack of gentleness) and 118 (lack of omniscience) do not seem to be auspicious, let alone wholly so.

The most straightforward explanation of the inconsistent nature of this list seems to me that the original enumeration of auspicious or meritorious mental events, given in order to elaborate on the statement made in verse 7, was later expanded by merging it with a larger general list of mental events, not all of which were auspicious. As is apparent from the following discussion, it is always presupposed that *all* the members of the list are auspicious by nature. For present purposes we will therefore ignore the inauspicious intruders.

It is evident that Nāgārjuna's opponent here adopts the perspective of an Ābhidharmika. Some scholars have taken this as an indication that Nāgārjuna is replying to different opponents in different parts of the text: in the present case he replies to a Buddhist, while the reply to verses 5 and 6 is directed at a Naiyāyika.[82] I consider the hypostasis of objections into objectors as not very helpful; at best it is useful as an expository device. But if we take this device too seriously, we will be forced to have an opinion on such questions as whether the opponent in verses 7 and 8 is really a Buddhist or merely a Naiyāyika provisionally adopting a theory of Nāgārjuna's co-religionists.[83] Apart from the obvious difficulty of ever settling this question, its answer also makes no difference for the assessment of Nāgārjuna's reply.

Thus the following are auspicious in one of their aspects: (1) cognition, (2) feeling, (3) discrimination, (4) volition, (5) touch, (6) attention, (7) aspiration, (8) devotion, (9) effort, (10) memory, (11) meditative stabilization, (12) wisdom, (13) equanimity, (14) practice, (15) complete practice, (16) attainment, (17) noble intention, (18) freedom from anger, (19) joy, (20) effort, (21) zeal, (22) connection

80. *kuśalamahābhūmika*, La Vallée Poussin (1988–1990: 189–193).
81. Johnston (1938: 315).
82. Bhattacharya et al. (1978: 39–40), Tucci (1929: xiii).
83. Bhattacharya et al. (1978: 100; note 2, 128).

with ignorance, (23) perseverance, (24) freedom from obstacles, (25) possession of power, (26) aversion, (27) absence of repentance, (28) grasping, (29) not grasping, (30) recollection, (31) firmness, (32) special adherence, (33) freedom from effort, (34) freedom from delusion, (35) freedom from exertion, (36) striving, (37) aspiration, (38) satisfaction, (39) being disjoint from the object, (40) being not conducive to liberation, (41) birth, (42) enduring, (43) impermanence, (44) possession, (45) old age, (46) utter torment, (47) dissatisfaction, (48) deliberation, (49) pleasure, (50) clarity, (51) grasping the discordant, (52) affection, (53) discordance, (54) grasping the concordant, (55) fearlessness, (56) reverence, (57) veneration, (58) devotion, (59) lack of devotion, (60) obedience, (61) respect, (62) lack of respect, (63) suppleness, (64) ebullience, (65) speech, (66) agitation, (67) attainment, (68) lack of faith, (69) lack of suppleness, (70) purification, (71) steadfastness, (72) gentleness, (73) repentance, (74) anguish, (75) confusion, (76) arrogance, (77) grasping the unfavourable, (78) doubt, (79) pure discipline, (80) inner serenity, (81) fear; moreover, there is (82) faith, (83) bashfulness, (84) rectitude, (85) being not deceived, (86) pacification, (87) being without fickleness, (88) conscientiousness, (89) kindness, (90) discriminating comprehension, (91) freedom from anger, (92) freedom from desire, (93) lack of self-infatuation, (94) lack of attachment, (95) lack of hatred, (96) lack of ignorance, (97) omniscience, (98) non-abandonment, (99) affluence, (100) modesty, (101) lack of concealment, (102) unobstructed intention, (103) compassion, (104) loving kindness, (105) non-discouragement, (106) absence of passion, (107) magical powers, (108) lack of attachment, (109) lack of envy, (110) a mind free from eradication, (111) patience, (112) renunciation, (113) lack of gentleness, (114) being in accordance with one's resources, (115) merit, (116) attainment of the state of non-conception, (117) being conducive to liberation, (118) lack of omniscience, (119) uncompounded phenomena.

In this way the 119 auspicious things have an auspicious substance. In the same way, the inauspicious things have an inauspicious substance; the obscured-neutral mental states are substantially obscured-neutral mental states; the non-obscured-neutral mental states[84] *are substantially non-obscured-neutral mental states; what is called desire has a substance that is called desire; what is called matter has a substance that is called matter; what is called immaterial has a substance that is called immaterial; uncontaminated things have an uncontaminated substance; what is called suffering, its origin, its cessation, and the path leading to cessation has a substance that is called suffering, its cessation, and the path leading to its cessation; that which is to be abandoned by meditation has a substance which is to be abandoned*

84. *prakṛtāvyākṛta.* I have not been able to trace this term. However, reconstructing from the Tibetan *ma bsgribs la lung du ma bstan pa*, we get *anivṛtāvyākṛta*, a term that is both found in numerous Abhidharma texts and fits in well with the pairs of opposites given here and in the commentary to the next verse.

by meditation; that which is not to be abandoned has a substance that is not to be abandoned.

After the list of 119 auspicious things, the commentary continues by noting that in the same way as auspicious mental events are intrinsically auspicious, the inauspicious ones are also inauspicious by nature. It then gives a list of further central notions of the Buddhist doctrine. All of the terms mentioned can be found in Abhidharma compendia such as Asaṅga's *Abhidharmasamuccaya* or Vasubandhu's *Abhidharmakośabhāṣya*. The obscured-neutral and non-obscured-neutral mental states are types of defiled and undefiled mental states, respectively. They are states that do not lead to karmic consequences and are therefore neither wrong conduct nor active right conduct. Desire (*kāma*), matter (*rūpa*), and the immaterial (*ārūpya*) point at the realm of desire (*kāmadhātu*), the realm of form (*rūpadhātu*), and the formless realm (*ārūpyadhātu*), which constitute three major divisions in Buddhist cosmology. "That which is to be abandoned by meditation" refers to mental obscuration which can only be eliminated by continuous meditative practice, as opposed to faults which can be eliminated by cognition alone.[85]

As far as different kinds of substances of things are evident in this way, the statement made in this context "All things are insubstantial, and because of insubstantiality they are empty" is not tenable.

The conclusion to be drawn from all these lists is that there are some objects which the Buddhist himself regards as auspicious or inauspicious. These objects have their characteristics by nature: that kindness is a meritorious mental state is not just a result of its causes or of some intersubjective convention by which we label it as meritorious. It has this quality intrinsically, in the same way as suffering is not only conventionally troublesome but has this property independent of what anybody thinks about suffering. And if this is true then at least the central terms of the Buddhist world-view refer to objects that are not empty, so that this world-view proves to be incompatible with the thesis of universal emptiness.

8. The phenomena of liberation have the substance of phenomena of liberation. The same holds for those things which have been mentioned in connection with the state of things, as well as for those things which are not phenomena of liberation.

This verse enlarges the list of items that supposedly have their qualities intrinsically. The "phenomena of liberation" (*nairyāṇika-dharma*) refer to entities associated with the last of the sixteen aspects of the four noble truths, liberation or definite deliverance (*nairyāṇika*). What the opponent wants to say is that those

85. These latter are called *darśanaprahātavyāḥ*. Frauwallner (1995: 158–159) lists errors and doubt among faults that can be eliminated by cognition alone, while the abandonment of passion, anger, and so forth requires meditative practice.

phenomena which make the Buddhist path a reliable means for attaining enlightenment have this property substantially. He then claims that the same is true of the objects referred to in the last verse as well as of the opposites of the phenomena of liberation.

Here things which have been mentioned in connection with the state of things, as well as those conducive to liberation, have a substance conducive to liberation. Those which are not conducive to liberation have a substance not conducive to liberation, the limbs of enlightenment have a substance which is the limbs of enlightenment, those which are not the limbs of enlightenment have a substance which is not the limbs of enlightenment, the factors harmonious with enlightenment have a substance which is harmonious with enlightenment, those which are not harmonious with enlightenment have a substance which is not harmonious with enlightenment. The same holds for the remaining ones.

The autocommentary here lists yet more categories from Buddhist thought which are supposed to be counterexamples to the theory of universal emptiness. All of them can be found in Asaṅga's *Abhidharmasamuccaya* as well as in the *Dharmasamgraha*, a short dictionary of Buddhist terms attributed to Nāgārjuna.[86] The "limbs of enlightenment" (*bodhyaṅgikaḥ*) comprise seven mental states (such as mindfulness, joy, and equanimity) intimately connected with the mind of an enlightened being, while the "factors harmonious with enlightenment" (*bodhipakṣikaḥ*) constitute a list of thirty-seven items which contains the seven limbs of enlightenment as well as a variety of other phenomena, such as the five sense-faculties and the eightfold noble path. The negatives of these categories are not to be understood as just any objects which are not identical with mindfulness, joy, and so forth but rather their specific opposites: lack of mindfulness, absence of joy, and so forth. The point being made is once again that these positive qualities accepted by the Buddhist doctrine have to be regarded as substantially positive, and their opposites as substantially negative. But once we have accepted that *some* objects have their qualities substantially and are therefore not empty, there is no reason to be squeamish about substances in general. Given his own doctrinal perspective, the opponent argues, the Buddhist would be better off adopting a theory that countenances substances, rather than with Nāgārjuna's thesis of universal emptiness.

So far as different kinds of substances of things are evident in this way, because of this the statement "All things are insubstantial, and because of insubstantiality they are empty" is not tenable.

Strangely enough, the final words of the autocommentary on the preceding verse are repeated here in almost the same way. Perhaps this repetitiveness

86. Kasawara et al. (1885).

results from the same cause which is responsible for the problems with the list of 119 auspicious things in the preceding verse.

REPLY

*52. **If people who know the state of things speak of the auspicious things, the auspicious substance should be expressed in terms of a detailed division.***

Those who know the state of things think that there is an auspicious substance of auspicious things, and this would have to be specified by you in terms of a detailed division: "This is the auspicious substance, these are the auspicious things, this is the consciousness of that auspicious thing, this is the substance of the consciousness of that auspicious thing." This would have to be done for all cases, but such a specification is not apparent. To this extent your statement "the substance of things has been specified individually" is not tenable.

Nāgārjuna points out in reply that up to now the opponent has not in fact given any argument apart from stating the undisputable fact that Buddhist doctrine considers some phenomena to be auspicious or meritorious and some inauspicious or not meritorious. What remains to be done, however, is to show that the claim that something is auspicious entails that there is an auspicious substance underlying it, that it is auspicious all by itself and does not derive its auspicious qualities from any other object. No such argument has been put forward yet.

In fact, the opponent could say more at this point than just stressing that the Ābhidharmikas themselves consider these phenomena to be substantially auspicious. He might try to establish the link between having a quality and having it substantially in the following way. Suppose that, for example, the sources of suffering referred to in the first noble truth—birth, old age, sickness, and death—did not have suffering as their intrinsic nature. In this case, it is not that they have the nature of suffering because of any property birth, old age, sickness, and death have from their own side, but that they are conceptualized in a particular way by human beings. If we cannot ground their unsatisfactoriness in the the phenomena themselves, we have to refer to some kind of convention that we all share, on the basis of which they are regarded as unsatisfactory. But then the objective of the Buddhist path loses much of its weight, since it now appears not to tackle a real problem (namely, the problem of the existence of suffering) but merely a problem of our own devising (the problem that we conceptualize things in a way which makes them appear to have the nature of suffering). The same, of course, applies to the positive attributes of a Buddha: they do not have any positive qualities in themselves but merely appear that way to beings with a particular cognitive setup. If the Buddha's four noble truths are not truths about the nature of things, but merely truths about conventions, like truths in a story that only function against a particular system of make-believe, they can have no force in convincing anyone who chooses not to adopt this system of conventions. In this way, the theory of emptiness swallows up key concepts of Buddhist thought and only returns impotent, convention-based substitutes. Because of this, anyone who takes the Buddhist doctrine seriously has to accept that the auspicious and inauspicious phenomena it talks about have their properties by nature, independent of our conceptualization of them.

53. ***And if the auspicious substance is produced based on conditions, how is this extrinsic nature of the auspicious things in fact a substance?***

If the substance of the auspicious things is produced in dependence on the collection of causes and conditions, how can there be a substance of the auspicious things produced from an extrinsic nature? It is just the same for the inauspicious things, and so forth. In this context, your statement "the auspicious substance of the auspicious things was explained, as was the the inauspicious substance, etc., of the inauspicious things, and so forth" is not tenable.

An immediate problem with regarding auspicious phenomena of the type just mentioned as substantially auspicious is the fact that they are causally produced. The qualities of buddhahood are something which is not there all the time but which is brought about through the practice of the Buddhist path. So they depend for their existence on other phenomena, namely, the set of practices one has to follow in order to become a Buddha.

For this to be a problem, the opponent must find it impossible to assert that the phenomena in question depend on causes and conditions and still exist substantially. This was not the view of the Ābhidharmikas in general, who did hold that substances such as primary existents (*dravya*) could interact in a causal network, and justified their status as independent existents in other ways (for example, by their not depending on their parts and by being independent of human interests or concerns).

But the opponent might be aware of the problem that follows if he accepts auspicious and inauspicious mental states as causally produced. Assume some set of practices now acts as the cause of an enlightenend mental state later on. As the enlightened state does not exist at present and the present state does not exist anymore when the enlightened state does, the relation of causation will always have one non-existent relatum. Our recollection of the past state or expectation of the future state will supply a substitute, so that we can conceptualize the relation between the two states in terms of a causal relation. But the fact that they are causally related is obviously not something with a mind-independent existence, since one of its relata is mind-dependent. It is a conceptual construct. If we assume that the nature of auspicious mental states involves a causal relation connecting them with earlier mental states, and if this causal relation is a conceptual construct, the auspicious mental states cannot be mind-independent, either. In order to keep the mind-dependent notion of causation from invading some of the central concepts of the Buddhist path and thereby threatening their objectivity, the opponent might consider it prudent to deny that they are causally produced. We can only speculate about how he might want to do this, but an obvious idea would be to claim that both the auspicious mental states of a Buddha as well as the inauspicious mental states are already fully present in our mind but obscured by other factors. What the Buddhist practices would do is merely to reveal these states, but not bring them about.

54. If the substance of the auspicious things was not produced in dependence on anything, there would be no religious practice.

Furthermore, you might think "the auspicious substance of the auspicious things is not produced in dependence on anything, nor is the inauspicious substance of the inauspicious things, nor the indeterminate substance of the indeterminate things. Therefore there is no religious practice." Why? Because this is the denial of dependent origination. And because dependent origination is denied, the apprehension of dependent origination is denied. This is because an apprehension of non-existent dependent origination cannot be obtained. And when there is no apprehension of dependent origination there is no apprehension of the true state of things. For the Blessed One said, "O Monks, whoever sees dependent origination sees the true state of things." Because there is no apprehension of the true state of things, there is no religious practice.

One difficulty with denying the causal origin of the mental states in question is that it is rather difficult to reconcile this with the key Buddhist teaching of dependent origination. Nāgārjuna here cites the *Śālistambasūtra*,[87] in which the Buddha asserts that the apprehension of the way things are originated in dependence on one another is equivalent not just to an understanding of the true nature of things but also to the apprehension of the Buddha himself. It is therefore hard to see how the opponent who takes his premisses from a Buddhist background can accept both the idea of dependent origination and the view that certain key items of the Buddhist worldview are not so originated.

On the other hand, one might argue for the same conclusion by saying that the denial of dependent origination entails the denial of the origin of suffering, as dependent origination is the origin of suffering. Because the origin of suffering is denied, suffering is denied. While there is no origin, from where will suffering arise? Because suffering and its origin are denied, the cessation of suffering is denied. While there is no origin of suffering, the destruction of what will be its cessation? While there is no cessation of suffering, what is to be obtained on a path that leads to the cessation of

87. Reat (1993: 27).

suffering? In this way the four noble truths do not exist. While these do not exist there is no fruit of religious practice, since this fruit is obtained by the apprehension of these truths. Because there are no such fruits, there is no religious practice.

If we assume that an inauspicious mental state such as suffering is not causally produced, this contradicts the second noble truth, that of the origin of suffering. The commentary also claims that we face a contradiction with the first noble truth, that of the existence of suffering, since if suffering is seen as uncaused it cannot have arisen from anywhere. But this only holds if we assume that everything is causally produced, an assumption the opponent need not share. Moreover, it is clear from his statements above that he does not deny the existence of auspicious and inauspicious mental states, such as suffering. But even if the first noble truth is accepted by the opponent, there will be a problem with the third one, that of the cessation of suffering. For if suffering is not part of the causal network, how can anything cause it to cease to exist? And if nothing can cause it to cease to exist, there is no path describing various techniques bringing this about, so the fourth noble truth, the truth of the path, has to be denied too.

It now appears that the opponent's worry, that Nāgārjuna's thesis of universal emptiness destroys the Buddhist path, applies to himself. Since the four noble truths form the very core of all Buddhist teachings, their negation, which is a consequence of assuming that the mental states in question are not causally produced, entails the negation of Buddhist practice altogether.

The discussion in this and in the following two verses has a close parallel in chapter 24 of the *Mūlamadhyamakakārikā*, which provides a detailed discussion of the connection between the notion of emptiness and the Buddhist path. This point is raised again at the very end of the *Vigrahavyāvartanī* in verse 70 (see section 3.10 below).

55. ***There would be neither right nor wrong nor worldly conventions. They would be permanent and substantial; because they are permanent they are acausal.***

While it is like this, which fault follows for you from the negation of dependent origination? "There is no right, there is no wrong, there are no worldly conventions." Why? Because as this is all dependently originated, when there is no dependent origination where should it come from?

If actions are right or wrong depending on whether they bring about auspicious or non-auspicious mental states, then right or wrong actions could not exist, since nothing can bring about the respective mental states. Systems of worldly conventions, such as the conventions of propriety, are put in place to regulate our behavior relative to right and wrong actions, and therefore depend on these. But if these do not exist, the conventions fail to connect with anything and therefore cease to be functional.

Also, what is substantial would not be dependently originated, but acausal and permanent. Why? Because acausal things are permanent. In this context, the non-existence of religious practice would follow exactly. And there is a contradiction with your own position. Why? Because the Blessed One said that all compounded things are impermanent. Hence they are permanent because they are substantially permanent.

If the opponent does not think that the auspicious and inauspicious mental states are part of the causal network, then nothing can bring them about and nothing can cause them to cease. In this case they would have to have existed for ever, and continue to do so in the future.[88] In this case, the Buddhist path would be pointless, as one could neither bring about the cessation of the inauspicious, such as suffering, or cultivate the auspicious, such as the qualities of a Buddha. A final difficulty, and one that will be decisive for the Buddhist opponent, is that his postulation of permanent mental qualities contradicts the Buddha's own teaching that all compounded phenomena are impermanent. In the *Aṅguttara-Nikāya*[89] we find the Buddha describing the "three characteristics" or "three seals" (*trilakṣaṇa, tilakkhaṇa*) of existence: all things are impermanent, suffering, and without self. It can be hardly satisfactory if the Buddhist opponent, trying to reject what he takes to be Nāgārjuna's excessive interpretation of the third seal in the thesis of universal emptiness, ends up contradicting the first.

56. Thus there is a difficulty for the inauspicious things, the indeterminate ones, those leading to liberation, and so forth. To this extent everything compounded is just not compounded for you.

The method which has been indicated with reference to the auspicious things is just the same for the inauspicious, for the indeterminate, for those leading to liberation, and so forth. To this extent, for you everything compounded becomes not compounded. Why? While there is no cause there is no arising, remaining, and decay. Because there is no characteristic of the compounded, in the absence of arising, remaining, and decay everything compounded becomes uncompounded. In this context, your statement "because auspicious things and so forth are endowed with substance all things fail to be empty" is not tenable.

As was pointed out above already, the opponent's point equally applies to the natures of all mental states considered in the Buddhist teachings, all of which would have to be regarded as having their respective natures substantially.[90] But

88. A possibility not mentioned here is that these mental states could pop in and out of existence without a cause. This would avoid the consequence of their permanence, but the resulting theory of non-causal change is hardly something this Buddhist opponent would want to accept. Nor, in fact, would anybody else, as Nāgārjuna argues elsewhere. See Westerhoff (2009a: 111–112).

89. 3:134; Woodward (1979: 1:264–265).

90. I read the expression "everything compounded" as a restricted generalization extending to the phenomena the opponent has mentioned as well as others like them. There is no need to take it to include other phenomena, such as material objects, as well.

as it was just argued that this implies their permanence, a reclassification of the these mental states would be implied. The Abhidharma ontology regards such states as uncompounded, but given the opponent's understanding of them as permanent, they would have to be grouped together with such uncompounded phenomena as space.[91] But this consequence is obviously not acceptable for an opponent who starts out by regarding the Abhidharma classification as authoritative.

It therefore turns out that far from being required by the Buddhist doctrine, regarding auspicious and inauspicious mental states as having their natures substantially actually undermines it, since it does not allow us to see how suffering could ever be removed or the qualities of Buddhahood obtained, unless we assume that these mental states are already present in our mind in some hidden form. But this will then conflict with the central Buddhist view of impermanence.

Regarding the four noble truths as akin to truths in a fiction need not cause any problems as long as we keep in mind how persistent the habits and conventions are that bind us to the fiction of cyclic existence in the first place. That something exists only by force of convention does not mean that we can change or abolish it at will. Few people will disagree that an institution like money only exists because a group of people act as if it did. But the fact that there is nothing in the world a fifty-pound note stands for does not imply that we can just create a positive balance in our bank account by stipulation. To this extent, the Buddhist doctrine can be regarded as a real solution to a real problem, even if suffering is not real to the extent that it reflects a mind-independent feature of reality.

3.4. Names without Objects [9, 57–59]

9. And if there was no substance, there would also not even be the name "insubstantiality of things," for there is no name without a referent.

And if the substance of all things were not to exist, there would be the absence of substance. There would also not be the name "absence of substance." Why? For there is no name whatsoever without a referent. Therefore, because the name exists, there is the substance of things, and because substance exists all things are non-empty. Therefore the statement "all things are without substance, because of being without substance they are empty" is not tenable.

To understand this criticism, we have to take into account the Nyāya theory of language the opponent has in mind here. The ontological theory this is

91. On the *asaṃskṛta-dharma* in Sarvāstivāda Abhidharma, see Dhammajoti (2004: chapter 16).

based on comes from the Vaiśeṣika school[92] and conceives of properties as separate entities over and above the individuals that instantiate them. We therefore regard an apple and the redness it instantiates as two distinct kinds of entities, neither of which is any more fundamental than the other.

This ontological picture is combined with a realist semantics in which there is a clear correspondence between the categories existing in the world, such as individuals, properties, and absences, and the expressions of language. The opponent refers to this when he claims that "there is no name without a referent." This position should not be misunderstood as saying that any name we come up with will be guaranteed to have a referent. The Naiyāyika is not obliged to believe in yetis just because our language contains the term "yeti." The point is, rather, that when we continue to unpack such a term along the lines of "large apelike creature supposedly inhabiting the Himalayas," we eventually end up with a description using only terms that have a referent. The Naiyāyika realism does not demand that each term has a referent, but merely that all of the simplest terms connect directly with the categories out there in the world.

The opponent argues that Nāgārjuna's use of the term "absence of substance" entails the existence of substance. Assuming that "substance" is one of the simplest terms in the language, it is guaranteed to refer to something out there in the world. When we speak about its absence, we can only mean its local absence, in the way in which blueness is absent from the red apple but present elsewhere.[93] Nāgārjuna's thesis of universal emptiness is therefore only true in a restricted sense, claiming that certain things do not have substances but that others do, or meaningless, if the term "substance" it employs does not refer to anything in the world.

REPLY

57. Where someone said "a name has a referent,"[94] one would say "then substance exists." You have to reply "we do not assert a name of this kind."

Where someone said "a name has a referent," one would say "then substance exists." You have to reply: "If there is a referring name of a substance it has to exist

92. Matilal (1968:16). In fact the association between the two schools Nyāya and Vaiśeṣika is so close that they are often referred to jointly by the name Nyāya-Vaiśeṣika. There is, however, little consensus on how the two schools came to be associated, and scholars even disagree on whether it would not be more satisfactory to speak of one school rather than of two.

93. For further discussion of this point, see section 3.6 below.

94. Bhattacharya (1978: 128) translates the term *sadbhūta* as "existent." I do not think that this is a particularly fortunate choice, since Nāgārjuna does not want to claim that emptiness entails a lack of existence. It appears to me that what Nāgārjuna wants to say is that if the Nyāya account was indeed correct and each simple term in a statement had to denote an existent object, there would be substances. But then saying that a name is *sadbhūta* would not mean that the name exists (which neither Nāgārjuna nor his opponent denies) but that it works in the way the Nyāya theory says it does: Each simple term is connected with its referent in the world.

due to the substantial referent. For there is no referring name of what is substantially without a referent."[95] *However, we do not assert a referring name. This is because a name, too, due to the absence of substance in things, is insubstantial and therefore empty. Because of its emptiness it is non-referring. In this context, your statement "because of being endowed with a name there is a substantial referent" is not tenable.*

Nāgārjuna replies by rejecting the semantic theory the opponent presupposes. The opponent's move from the use of the term "substance" to the existence of what the term refers to only works against the background of the specific theory of meaning assumed. For the opponent, if there is a referring name of a substance, this substance has to exist because the substantial referent exists. Something which is substantially without a referent, as for example the concept "horn of a hare" or "son of a barren woman" cannot be picked out by a referring name. If "substance" was an empty concept, we could not speak about it on the basis of the Nyāya theory of language.

However, Nāgārjuna does not see any reason for coupling his theory of emptiness with a Nyāya-style realist semantics. He does not have to assume that simple terms are guaranteed to have a referent in the way the Naiyāyika says they do, or indeed that names refer at all. By adopting a different theory of language, the problem the opponent described in verse 9 can be circumvented.

58. The name "non-existent"—what is this, something existent or again something non-existent? For if it is existent or if it is non-existent, either way your position is deficient.

And this name "non-existent," is that existent or non-existent? For if it is the name of an existent, or if it is the name of a non-existent, in both cases the thesis is deficient. If in this context the name "non-existent" is the name of an existent, to that extent the thesis is abandoned. For it is not the case that something is now non-existent, now existent. Moreover, if the name 'non-existent' is the name of a non-existent—there is no name of something which does not exist. To that extent, the thesis "the name exists substantially, so there is a substantial referent of the name," is deficient.

This verse describes a dilemma for the type of realist semantics defended by the opponent. Consider the referent of the term "non-existent." If it is an existent referent, then the statement we want to make encounters a problem, since we are now dealing with some object which *ex hypothesi* does exist and at the same time does not exist, since it is the worldly counterpart of the term "non-existent." On the other hand, its referent cannot be non-existent, since the realist does not allow for (simple) terms in the language that have no referent.

95. The Sanskrit has *iti* after this sentence, indicating the end of the statement introduced by "you have to reply." It makes better sense, however, to follow the Tibetan and omit this, since the "you" is a Madhyamaka. His reply is then taken to begin with the words "If there is a referring name . . ." and continues until the end of the autocommentary on this verse.

Whichever horn of the dilemma we adopt, it seems impossible to make sense of the meaning of the term "non-existent." But since its meaning is perfectly clear to us, this indicates that there is something wrong with the realist semantics presupposed.

What a contemporary semantic realist would want to reply here is that this problem can be solved if we regard "non-existent" as a second-order predicate. The semantics for a sentence like "yetis are non-existent" is then to be spelled out in terms of the second-order property of being uninstantiated applying to the first-order property of being a yeti. We can also seize the first horn of the dilemma in asserting that the second-order property of being uninstantiated is itself instantiated (since there is such a property). It is only applicable to first-order properties, but does not apply to itself; in fact, the theory of types which forms part of such a semantics usually excludes that properties can apply to themselves.

It is not entirely clear whether the realist will be happy with this, however. After all, this solution comes at the price of splitting up the property "is non-existent" into infinitely many properties "is uninstantiated," each of which only applies to objects at certain level in the type-theoretic hierarchy (first-order properties, second-order properties, and so forth). If we want to hold that there is just *one* such property rather than infinitely many resembling ones, this solution will not be attractive to us.

59. The emptiness of all things was presented earlier. To this extent, this is a criticism of a non-thesis.

The emptiness of all things was presented here in detail by our earlier remarks. The emptiness of the name has been asserted above, as well. Having adopted the non-emptiness of things, you replied to this "if the substance of things did not exist there would be no name 'non-substance.'" So far your criticism amounts to a criticism of a non-thesis, because we do not say that there is a referring name.

This verse emphasizes once again the point made in verse 57. As Nāgārjuna asserts a thesis of *universal* emptiness, it should be clear that the constituents of language are subsumed under this as well. It would indeed be problematic to combine Nāgārjuna's theory with a Nyāya-style realist semantics. But as Nāgārjuna does not want to do this, the difficulty described in verse 9 does not present a problem for him.

3.5. Extrinsic Substances [10, 60]

10. Rather, substance exists, yet the substance of things does not exist. It has to be explained to what this thingless substance belongs.

You might rather think: "Let there not be a name without referent. Substance is produced, but the substance of things is not brought about in turn. In this way the emptiness of things will be established because of the absence of substance of things. And there is no name without referent."

The opponent now makes a suggestion how Nāgārjuna's theory of emptiness could be combined with a realist semantics. Suppose Nāgārjuna's arguments against the substances of things are accepted. In this case there will be no substance, but even if this is so and there are no substances *of things*, this does not necessarily have to imply that there are no substances whatsoever. There could be other substances, and these would then act as the referents of linguistic expressions. In this way we would not have to give up the intuitively plausible thesis that there is something out there in the world our language connects with, while at the same time agreeing to the Nāgārjunian criticism of the notion of substance.

Here we say: The object to which the thingless substance of the object belongs needs to be explained. But this is not explained. So far the assumption "substance exists but this in turn is not the substance of things" is deficient.

The opponent points out that if Nāgārjuna is going to accept his suggestion, he has to give us a bit more detail at this point. In particular we need an account of what exactly this substance which is now supposed to exist is like. It is clear it cannot be part of the world, as it would otherwise fall prey to Nāgārjuna's arguments against substance. But since it is at the same time supposed to provide the referents of our language, this also implies that what we are talking about is not part of the world, either. When we seem to be speaking about the pot in front of us, the pot cannot be the referent, because it is empty. If the reference of the term "pot" to something out there is then guaranteed by some other substance located elsewhere, it turns out that we are systematically deceived about what our language refers to. As Nāgārjuna has not really given us any details on how this supposed fix is to work, it cannot be regarded as a satisfactory reply to the problem raised in verse 9.

REPLY

60. "Substance exists and it is not a substance of things"—the worry expressed there is no worry.

This is because we do not negate the substance of things, or assert the substance of some object distinct from things. While this is so, is it not that your criticism "if things are without substance, now the substance of which other object distinct from things is there? It would be right if this was pointed out" disappears from view and is in fact no criticism at all.

Even though the first sentence of the autocommentary contains the word "or," it might make more sense to read it as containing an "and." Nāgārjuna does not want to say that he does *neither* of two things (negate the substance of things, assert the substance of some object distinct from things), since he definitely does the first. It appears that he rather wants to say that he does not do *both*: say there is no substance in things and assert the existence of some other kind of substance elsewhere.

In this case, Nāgārjuna also does not have to supply the details of the opponent's two-substance theory. There is no need to introduce a second kind of substance that is somehow immune from Nāgārjuna's arguments to assure us that we can still have a realist semantics. This is because we can do without a realist semantics in the first place. In particular, Nāgārjuna's own assertion that there is no substance is not to be interpreted on the basis of such a theory. If Nāgārjuna's own statements do not presuppose such a semantics, it is also not necessary to save the consistency of the theory by the rather desperate move of introducing "substances apart from things." Its consistency is only threatened if we combine it with the kind of Nyāya-style realist semantics Nāgārjuna has just rejected.

3.6. Negation and Existence [11–12, 61–64]

11. To the extent to which the negation "there is no pot in the house" is precisely a negation of an existent, your negation is a negation of an existing substance.

In this case the negation of an existent object, not of a non-existent one, is brought about. Thus the statement "there is no pot in the house" brings about the negation of an existent, not of a non-existent pot. Just in this way, the statement "there is no substance of things" achieves the negation of an existent substance, not of a non-existent one. In this context, the statement "All things are insubstantial, and because of insubstantiality they are empty" is not tenable. Precisely because the negation is brought about, the substance of all things is not refuted.

The thesis of universal emptiness is a negative thesis, as it asserts that substance does not exist anywhere. It is therefore particularly important to get a clear idea of how Nāgārjuna understands the interpretation of negated statements.

In this criticism the opponent assumes that Nāgārjuna holds the Nyāya view of negation. As we recall from the discussion of verse 9, the Naiyāyika holds that all the simple terms in a sentence must refer to some objects in the world. In addition, the Naiyāyikas regard the absence of a property as a category in its own right, as something that can equally be instantiated by an individual, just as a property can. In this way, the red apple can be seen both as related to redness by instantiation as well as to blueness by absence.

Presupposing for the sake of argument that all terms in the statement "There is no pot in the house" are simple, the Naiyāyika will then take its referent to be the individual pot standing in the absence relation to the house. Understood in this way, both affirmative and negative judgments involve a qualification or attribution, either an attribution via an instantiation relation or an attribution via an absence relation.

Since the Naiyāyika presupposes that in a meaningful statement all simple terms must refer, negative statements will have to be understood as local absences. For "There is no pot in the house" to be meaningful, there must be a pot somewhere that can be related to the house by an absence relation. The sentence must therefore be understood to assert the absence of the pot in the house together with its presence somewhere else. Similarly, a sentence like "This apple is not red" will claim the local absence of red, together with its presence elsewhere.

It is now obvious how we run into problems if we apply this understanding of negation to any of Nāgārjuna's statements which claims that some object lacks a substance. Since it is imperative for the Naiyāyika that all of the terms have to refer for the sentence to be meaningful, such a sentence, if true, must assert the absence of substance in the object considered, *together with its presence somewhere else.* But Nāgārjuna has explicitly ruled out the appeal to any second kind of substance which is deemed to exist in order to provide a reference for the terms "substance" in verse 60. Without this move, the individual statements appear to contradict the thesis of universal emptiness. Once again, the falsity of Nāgārjuna's claim seems to follow from the assumption that his assertions are meaningful.

REPLY

61. If negation is of an existent thing, is it not that emptiness is established? Because you negate the insubstantiality of things.

If negation is of an existent thing and not of a non-existent one, and if you negate the insubstantiality of all things, is it not that the insubstantiality of all things is established? Your speech, which is a negation, establishes emptiness because it is the negation of the insubstantiality of all things.

Unfortunately for the opponent, his criticism also works the other way round. For the opponent's own statement "universal emptiness does not exist" has to be false if it is to be regarded as meaningful. According to the opponent's own semantics, the term "emptiness" needs to have some counterpart in the real world for the statement to be meaningful. But if there is such a counterpart, emptiness will exist after all, so that the opponent's statement is false.

62. Or, if you negate emptiness and that emptiness does not exist, is your statement that "negation is of an existent thing" then not abandoned?

Or, if you negate the insubstantiality and emptiness of all things, and if that emptiness does not exist, now in that case your thesis that "negation is of an existing thing, not of a non-existing thing" is abandoned.

On the other hand, if we presuppose that the statement "universal emptiness does not exist" is true, then it cannot be meaningful, as one of its terms is now lacking a referent. So it seems as if the opponent is caught in the very same bind as the Mādhyamika.

63. I do not negate anything, and there is nothing to be negated. To this extent you misrepresent me when you say "you negate."

If I negated anything, then what you said would be appropriate. But I do not negate anything, since there is not anything to be negated. Therefore, while all things are empty, while the object of negation and the negation do not exist, you introduce a misrepresentation by saying "you negate."

How are we going to get out of this difficulty where each side is accusing the other of saying something false (if meaningful) or meaningless (if true)? The answer is that the problem was caused by attempting to couple Nāgārjuna's thesis of universal emptiness with a Naiyāyika semantics. It has now become thoroughly clear that this cannot work. Nāgārjuna therefore rejects this semantic theory and asserts that his negations of substance cannot be be interpreted along Nyāya lines. He therefore does not negate anything *according to the Nyāya understanding of negation*. This is because there is no substance out there which could serve as a referent of the term "substance" in a denial that there is such a thing. If we adopt the Nyāya semantics, then indeed Nāgārjuna does not negate anything. However, this is a good reason to attempt to do without this particular kind of semantics.

We might ask ourselves at this point why Nāgārjuna does not give a relatively obvious reply to the Nyāya worry about negative statements involving the notion of substance. This reply would be to state that substance is not a simple term of the language. As we noted earlier, the Naiyāyika has a way of asserting that there are no yetis, simply by rephrasing the reference to the supposedly non-existent entity in terms of expressions referring to existent qualities that do not occur together (such as "large apelike creature" and "inhabiting the Himalayas"). In a similar way, we could rephrase statements about substance as statements about properties that are instantiated, such as various causal and conceptual dependence relations. In this way, negating the existence of substance would just boil down to the assertion that no object is qualified by the absence of all these dependence relations at the same time.

In this way, we can address the Naiyāyika's worry, but it is questionable whether this is a position Nāgārjuna would want to adopt. The way the Naiyāyika interprets this answer still implies that there is a world of objectively existent properties which the most simple terms in our language refer to. While we would be able to make the statement "there are no substances" intelligible to the Naiyāyika, we would do so on the basis of a semantics very much unlike the one Nāgārjuna wants to introduce. The above reply is therefore one that Nāgārjuna would be reluctant to make, at least without significant further qualifications.

12. Now as this substance does not exist, what is negated by that statement of yours? For the negation of a non-existent is accomplished without words.

As this substance does indeed not exist, what do you negate by that statement "All things are insubstantial"? For the negation of a non-existent is established without words; it is like that for the coolness of fire or the solidity[96] *of water.*

In this objection, the opponent draws a distinction between two kinds of negation, one of which is established without words and one with words. Examples of the former are "there is no cool fire" and "there is no solid water." What constitutes a negation established with words is not stated explicitly, but we can assume that "regular" negations like "the pot is not in the house" are subsumed under this term. What makes negations like "there is no cool fire" irregular is the fact that the object negated is never encountered in our world. We never come across a cool fire or solid water; on the other hand, there are plenty of pots located in houses.

The opponent might therefore want to say that negations like "there is no pot in the house" have to be established linguistically because they negate a situation we are likely to encounter in the world. That fire is not cool and that water cannot be walked on, however, already becomes evident on close inspection of the respective natures of fire and water. We therefore do not need the statements "there is no cool fire" and "there is no solid water" to establish these negations. In fact, we *could* not even use words to express them because of the Nyāya theory of negation. We recall that for the Naiyāyika, terms used in negative sentences are all referential. What the negation expresses is the fact that these referents are not combined in the situation under discussion. The pot is not in the house, but in the garden or somewhere else; the apple is not red, but redness is instantiated in a rose or a red cloth. But in order to negate that the coolness of fire is to be found at some place, we would have to use a term that does not refer (always assuming that "coolness of fire" is a simple term),[97] thereby rendering the entire statement meaningless.

The opponent therefore objects here that if Nāgārjuna's theory of universal emptiness is not meaningless, since it is possible to establish negations of

96. The manuscript has *sthairyasya* (Yonezawa 2008: 242:5); Sāṅkṛtyāyana reconstructed from the Tibetan *chu la tsha ba nyid* to *apām auṣṇyasya* "the burning of water." The philosophical point remains unaffected.

97. If we did not make this assumption, the sentence could just be understood as asserting an absence relation of coolness in the fire and would therefore be unproblematic from the Nyāya point of view.

non-existent objects without words, it is at the very least pointless to assert it, in the same way in which it is pointless to assert that there is no cool fire, as if this was a real possibility one might encounter. If Nāgārjuna is right, then we have no more chance of coming across a substantial object than we have coming across a pool of solid water. There is thus no point in asserting the negation of either.

REPLY

64. Regarding your assertion that "expressing the negation of a non-existent object is accomplished without speech": in our case speech makes the non-existent known, it does not refute it.

When you say "the negation of a non-existent is also accomplished without speech," what does your statement "all things are insubstantial" do?' We reply: indeed, this statement "all things are insubstantial" does not make all things insubstantial. Nevertheless, while there is no substance, it makes known that "things are insubstantial."

In the same way, suppose someone said, while Devadatta is absent from the house, "Devadatta is in the house" and someone would reply, "he is not." That statement does not bring about the non-existence of Devadatta, but it only makes the absence of Devadatta in the house known. Likewise, that statement "there is no substance of things" does not bring about the insubstantiality of things, nevertheless it makes the absence of substance in all things known.

Moreover, all things lack substance, like an illusory person. Because they are ignorant of the lack of a real core in persons, stupid and ignorant childish beings superimpose a substance onto them. If there is no substance, the non-existence of substance is definitely established even without words or excluding words, because words bring about the understanding that things lack substance.[98]

In this context, your earlier statement "when there is no substance, what does that statement 'there is no substance' do? The absence of substance is also established without words" is not tenable.

The connection between the objection in verse 12 and this reply might not be immediately apparent. So let us take matters one step at a time. We remember that in verse 12 the opponent asserted that if it is the negation of a non-existent object we are concerned with, it is not necessary to establish it using language, since the things negated are not real possibilities we are ever likely to encounter. But the converse of this is just to say that because it is apparently necessary for Nāgārjuna to use language to establish his negation of substance, we cannot be dealing with the negation of a non-existent object. But if we are dealing with an existent object, that is, if Nāgārjuna's theory of

98. This paragraph is only found in the Tibetan translation (Yonezawa 2008: 319:13–20).

emptiness negates an existent substance, then this negation must somehow be able to make substance non-existent, since otherwise a negation of an existent object would simply be false.

The view that it is the theory of emptiness which somehow brings it about that all things lack substance is a misunderstanding addressed frequently in the Buddhist philosophical discussion.

The *Āryaratnakūṭasūtra* notes that:

> Things are not made empty by emptiness, but things are indeed empty. Things are not made to lack characteristics (*animitta*) by the fact that they lack characteristics, but things indeed lack characteristics.[99]

Tāranātha's history of Buddhism in India reports three questions concerning the Prajñāpāramitā literature which a King Gambhīrapakṣa asked Asanga. The last of these asks:

> When it is said that emptiness itself does not make everything empty, what is it that does not do so, and what is the cause of not doing so?[100]

A generalization of the view that denying the existence of substance makes substance non-existent is that negations somehow cause the negated thing to go out of existence. Peculiar as this position may seem, it was certainly considered by several Indian authors, even though none of them seem to have adopted it.[101] Uddyotakara points out that:

> negation does not have the power to make an existing thing otherwise [i.e., non-existent]. Because it makes something known it does not cause the existence of something to cease; [therefore] this negation [too] makes something known and does not cause the existence of something to cease.[102]

This view of negation, and of emptiness in particular, is of course rejected by Nāgārjuna. It is interesting to note that Candrakīrti, commenting in his *Bhāṣya* on *Madhyamakāvatāra* 6:34, which deals with a related issue, remarks that we

99. This passage is quoted in Candrakīrti's *Prasannapadā*: *yan na śūnyatayā dharmān śūnyān karoti | api tu dharmā eva śūnyāḥ | yan na animittena dharmān animittān karoti | api tu dharmā eva animittāḥ* (La Vallée Poussin 1903–1913: 248:4–5). Nakamura (1987:210) notes that this text was "in vogue" in the third to fifth century, but that its core existed already at the time of Nāgārjuna. See also verses 391–392 of Āryadeva's *Catuḥśataka* (Rinchen 1994:296).

100. *stong pa nyid kyis chos thams cad stong pa nyid du mi byed par bshad pa'i mi byed mkhan dang / mi byed rgyu'i stong nyid gang yin* (Schiefner 1868: 89:21–90:1).

101. Such as Patañjali commenting on 2.2.6 of Pāṇini's *Aṣṭādhyāyī* (Kielhorn 1880–1885: 411–412).

102. In his *Vārttika* on Vātsyāyana's *Bhāṣya* on *Nyāyasūtra* 2, 1, 11: *na ca pratiṣedhasyaitat sāmarthyaṃ yad vidyamānaṃ padārtham anyathā kuryat jñāpakatvāc ca na saṃbhavanivṛttiḥ jñāpako 'yaṃ pratiṣedho na saṁbhavanivartaka iti.* (Gautama 1887: 191:13–15), (Jha 1984: II:619).

must not think of emptiness as acting on substances along the lines of a hammer acting on a clay pot, that is, by assuming that it destroys something that is already there.[103]

Nevertheless, there are at least some Nyāya interpreters who suggest an understanding of negation in precisely this way. For example, we read in Phaṇibhūṣana's subcommentary on Vātsyāyana's commentary on the *Nyāyasūtra* concerning the negation of non-existent objects that:

> the very attempt to deny their existence presupposes the admission of their existence inasmuch as there is no sense in demolishing the possible existence of something which has no existence at all, just as it is impossible to smash with a stick the jar which does not exist.[104]

It appears that this passage does understand negation along the lines of the destruction of an already existent object, an interpretation that is used here to support the familiar Nyāya prohibition against the negation of non-existents.

Be this as it may, it is clear that Nāgārjuna rejects any interpretation of the denial of substance as bringing about the non-existence of substance. Nāgārjuna does indeed regard it as necessary to use words to establish his theory of universal emptiness—this is why he composed such treatises as the *Mūlamadhyamakakārikā*, the *Vigrahavyāvartanī*, and others. But this does not imply, as the opponent holds, that he is therefore attempting to negate an existent object, and would thus have to assume that his negations somehow destroyed this existent object. All Nāgārjuna's negations do is to make it known that there is no substance, as the statement that Devadatta is not in the house only makes it known that he is not there, but does not cause his absence. And this is indeed sufficient, since Nāgārjuna does not attempt to destroy an existent substance by his philosophical theorizing (an attempt that would be doomed to failure from the start) but merely the mistaken superimposition of such a substance onto a world which in fact lacks it.

In this way, Nāgārjuna can also reply to the objection from verse 12 that the theory of emptiness is pointless, since according to his own understanding substance does not just fail to exist but could not possibly exist. But even though substances are no more encountered in the world than samples of solid water, substance still constitutes a mistaken projection read into things that do not have substantial existence. For this reason, negating substance does have a point, just

103. *de'i phyir ji ltar tho ba la sogs pa dag bum pa la sogs pa rnams kyi 'jig pa'i rgyu yin pa de bzhin du/stong pa nyid kyang dngos po'i rang bzhin la skur pa'i gyur 'gyur ba zhig na de ni rung ba yang ma yin te* (La Vallée Poussin 1912: 117:15–18).

104. Chattopadhyaya and Gangopadhyaya (1968: 2:26).

as there would be a point in stating "there is no solid water" in front of people who suffered from frequent hallucinations of water one can walk on.

3.7. The Mirage Analogy [13–16, 65–67]

13. As ignorant people wrongly perceive water in a mirage, in the same way there would be a wrong perception for you in this case, for a non-existent object is negated.

In this verse, the opponent suggests another way of getting around the difficulty of the negation of a non-existent object discussed in the previous verses. We assume that the referent of the term in question is a deceptive appearance. The term is thereby meaningful, since there is something corresponding to it, yet at the same time we can negate it as long as we understand the negation to mean that the referent does not exist in the way it appears.

The example of a deceptive appearance the opponent uses is that of a mirage. This example is well known in the Buddhist philosophical literature. The Buddha himself used it as an illustration of the insubstantiality of the objects of perception.[105] It is frequently given as one of the "examples of illusion" in the Prajñāpāramitā literature that provide different illustrations of the ways phenomena are like an illusion. The *Mahāprajñāpāramitāśāstra*, a massive commentarial work that is sometimes attributed to Nāgārjuna, explicitly compares travelers deceived by a mirage to men ignorant of the emptiness of all things.[106] Later Buddhist philosophers such as Āryadeva and Vasubandhu also employ it in their discussions.

You might think: "Ignorant people wrongly perceive water in a mirage, and the learned ones say 'surely this mirage is waterless' in order to dispel this perception. In the same way the statement 'all things are insubstantial' is made in order to dispel the beings' perception of substance in things without substance."

In this way Nāgārjuna's assertion "the substance of things does not exist" could be interpreted along the lines of "the water in the mirage does not exist." There is no substance, just as there is no water. Nevertheless, our statements are meaningful because there is the appearance of substance and the appearance of water. The aim of Nāgārjuna, just as that of the guide in the desert, is to correct an error his deluded companions made. For this it is not necessary to assume that the terms "water in the mirage" or "substance in things" actually refer to anything; it is sufficient that the people at whom the statement is directed think they do.

105. In the *Phena Sutta*; Feer (1884–1898:3:141), Bodhi (2000:951).
106. Lamotte (1944–:1:363).

Here we say:

14. Yet, while it exists in this way, there are these six things: the perception, the perceived, and the perceiver of that object; the negation, the object of negation, and the negator.

If it is thus, there is indeed the perception by beings, there is the perceived, and there are those beings who perceive that object. There is also the negation of what is wrongly perceived, there is the object of negation, which is just the wrongly perceived object, and the negators of that perception, people like you; these six things are established. Because these six things are established, the statement "All things are empty" is not tenable.

The difficulty with interpreting Nāgārjuna's thesis of universal emptiness along the line of the denial of water in a mirage is that we now have to accept the existence of six different things:

1. The perception: Even if there is no water in the mirage there is certainly the perception of water in it. This is what makes a mirage a mirage.
2. The perceived: This is whatever it is that causes the perception. In this case it is obviously not water, but light rays bent as they pass through layers of air with different temperatures.
3. The perceiver: There must be somebody there who mistakes the perception of the bent light rays for water. Otherwise there would be no mirage.
4. The negation: The negation of the appearance (the statement of the guide) must exist, given the way the example is set up.
5. The negated: The negation must be the negation of some existing thing, in our case the water appearing in the mirage.
6. The negator: Finally we need someone who maintains the negation—in our example this is the guide in the desert.

For an illusion to work, at least some things must be truly existent. Even if there is no water in the mirage, what is perceived as water (the bent light rays) cannot be illusory, too. An illusion must be founded on reality somewhere; it cannot be illusions all the way down. A special case of this worry was raised by the opponent in the first two verses when he proposed the dilemma concerning the status of Nāgārjuna's thesis of universal emptiness. This point is made here again, as the opponent argues that the negation of the appearance must be real, even though the appearance is not. In the same way in which we can only have a mirage if at least some of the six items mentioned are not illusory in turn, just so Nāgārjuna's thesis of universal emptiness would presuppose the existence of something not empty. As this would show that Nāgārjuna's thesis is wrong, we therefore have to conclude that the example of the mirage is not a satisfactory way of spelling out what Nāgārjuna has in mind. Given the prominence of the example of a mirage as an illustration of emptiness in the Prajñāpāramitā literature, this would indeed be problematic, and could even be construed as an argument that Nāgārjuna does not faithfully represent the doctrine set forth in these scriptures.

15. But if there is just no perception, no perceived, and no perceiver, then there is certainly no negation, no object of negation, and no negator.

But by making the statement "there should not be that fault," while there just is no perception, no perceived, and no perceiver according to this, the negation of the perception, namely, "all things are insubstantial" does also not exist; there is also no object of negation, there is also no negator.

If, on the other hand, we assume that the mirage perceived, its perceptual causes, and its perceiver do not exist, there will be no object negated, because negation needs something to operate on. But then there will also be no statement truly expressing the negation of this object, nor will there be a negator, or at least nobody who can be described as a negator.

16. While there is neither negation, object of negation, nor negator, all things are established, and so is their substance.

While there is no negation, no object of negation, and no negator, all things are unnegated and the substance of all things exists.

If there is no negation of an appearance, no negated appearance, and no negator of an appearance, then there is also nothing which could negate the appearing substance. As such, the substance has to be assumed to exist.

REPLY

65. By the example of the mirage, you once again brought up an important discussion. In this context, too, you should listen to the demonstration of how this example is suitable.

You once again brought up a great discussion by the example of the mirage. In this context, too, the demonstration of how this example is suitable should be heard.

Unlike other examples suggested by the opponent (such as that of the self-illuminating fire in the commentary on verse 33), Nāgārjuna here agrees that this is useful for illustrative purposes. But it has to be explained properly to avoid the difficulties the opponent just mentioned. This is what Nāgārjuna is now going to do.

66. If perception existed substantially, it would not be dependently produced. The perception which is dependent, however, is it not precisely emptiness?

If the perception of water in a mirage was substantial, it would not be dependently originated. As far as it is produced dependent on the mirage, dependent on the mistaken vision, and dependent on the irregular mental activity, it is dependently arisen. And because it is dependently arisen therefore it is empty of substance. It is as was said earlier.

If Nāgārjuna asserts that the perception of water in the mirage (the first of the six items listed above) exists, he does not mean that it exists substantially. The water in the mirage is a perfect example of something that does not exist from its own side but purely in dependence on other things, such as refracted light rays and the way these are processed in vision and subsequently classified as perceptions of water. As such, mirages do not present a counterexample to Nāgārjuna's thesis of universal emptiness but a good example of how dependent things exist.

67. If perception existed substantially, who would remove the perception? As far as the same pattern applies to the remaining cases this is a non-criticism.

If the perception of water in the mirage existed substantially, who exactly would remove it? This is because substance, like the heat of fire, the wetness of water, the spaciousness of space, cannot be removed. But its removal is perceived. So far perception is empty of substance. Similarly, it has to be understood clearly that the same procedure applies to the remaining cases as well, the five beginning with the object perceived. In this context your statement "because there is the set of six all things are not empty" is not tenable.

If there really was perception-independent water in the mirage, we would not be able to remove it with actions that only affect our sensory capacities. The mirage's water ceases to exist if we change our point of view, or put on polarizing sunglasses. But the heat of a flame does not cease to exist if we insulate our perceptual capacities against it, for example by wearing fire-proof gloves. How do we know this? Because even if we do not perceive the heat because of the insulating power of the glove, this heat can still affect other things, it can burn a piece of paper or boil a kettle of water. But it is not the case that once we put on the polarizing sunglasses there continues to be water that can quench our thirst or sustain the life of fish, even though we cannot see it.

It is important to note in this context that when Nāgārjuna refers to qualities like the heat of fire, the wetness of water, and so on, as *svabhāva*, he does not want to claim that these exist substantially. The notion of *svabhāva* is here used to refer to an object's *essential* qualities. Thus heat constitutes the *svabhāva* of fire since this is a property the fire cannot lose without ceasing to be that very thing. Nevertheless, neither fire nor anything else exists substantially (*svabhāvatas*).[107]

107. Compare Candrakīrti's comments in the *Prasannapadā*; La Vallée Poussin (1903–1913:241:8–9, 260: 9–13). Further discussion of the different senses of *svabhāva* can be found in Westerhoff (2009a, chapter 2).

So even though neither the mirage's water nor the fire's heat exists substantially, the former is in a way even less substantial than the latter. That the perception of water in a mirage is not veridical at the level of day-to-day interaction can be inferred from its dependence on a single sensory modality, namely vision. Phenomena that can be veridically perceived at the level of day-to-day interaction, such as the heat of fire and the wetness of water, have causal powers apart from their ability to cause a certain perception in us.

We should note that even though it is true for Nāgārjuna to say that the perception of the mirage exists in some sense, this talk should in no way be understood in an ontologically serious manner. Nāgārjuna does not argue for the reality of appearances as some undubitable foundation that is impossible to question. Talk of appearances is pragmatically useful, but the mere usefulness of some set of terms does not indicate the existence of substantially existent referents of these terms. In fact, it is hard to understand how an appearance could possibly exist "from its own side"—such a thing could not be what we mean by the term "appearance."[108] In the same way in which we can speak of the perception of a mirage, we can talk about the perceived object, the perceiver, the negation, the object negated, and the negator. However, all of these only exist in a manner of speaking, but not substantially so. They all stand in dependence relations and are therefore empty.

3.8. Emptiness and Reasons [17–19, 68]

17. Your reason is not established. Because there is no substance, where then does your reason come from? Moreover, no matter is established without a reason.

The reason for your statement "all things are without substance" is not established. Why? Because of the lack of substance, all things are empty. Therefore, where does the reason come from? While there is no reason, where does the establishment of the statement "all things are empty," which is without reason, come from? In this context, the statement "all things are empty" is not tenable.

The opponent raises once again a now familiar objection, which in this instance focuses on the reason (*hetu*), a part of the standard Nyāya form of logical inference. The reason Nāgārjuna gives for his thesis of universal emptiness is, of course, the fact that all things are dependently originated. But if this reason is empty, too, the opponent argues, how is it going to function as a support in an argument for Nāgārjuna's thesis?

108. See Wood (1994: 265).

18. And if the denial of substance is established for you without a reason, the existence of substantiality is also established for me without a reason.

If you thought: "the insubstantiality of things is established without reason," then as far as the denial of substance is established for you without a reason, so far the existence of substance is also established for me without a reason.

It would not do to accept the opponent's criticism of the absence of a reason but to say that no such reason is necessary to establish Nāgārjuna's theory of universal emptiness. If Nāgārjuna is allowed to operate outside of the commonly accepted standards of rational argumentation, so is his opponent. He will then be similarly justified in asserting that substances do exist and could not be expected to produce a reason for this assertion.

19. If the reason exists, the "absence of substance of things" fails to be accomplished. For nowhere in the world is there anything without substance.

In this context, if you thought that the reason exists, the "insubstantiality of all things" fails to be accomplished. Why? For in the world there is no thing which is without substance.

After deriving an unacceptable consequence from the assumption that there is no need for a reason to establish Nāgārjuna's thesis of universal emptiness, the opponent now considers what follows if we do assume that the reason exists. Since he holds that existence entails substantial existence, the existence of the reason will provide a counterexample to Nāgārjuna's view that everything is without substance. And if Nāgārjuna's thesis is refuted, the insubstantiality he posits is to be found nowhere in the world. For this reason, Nāgārjuna can neither hold that there is a reason establishing his thesis, nor hold that there is none.

The interpretation I have given here follows the rendering in Bhattacharya et al.,[109] which also accords with the paraphrase in Mookerjee,[110] as well as with the way Yamaguchi[111] reads the Tibetan, and Tucci[112] the Chinese translation. It is, however, not the only way to understand the Sanskrit.[113] Bhattacharya[114] offers a different interpretation, translating as follows:

> ***Nor can you hold that the things' being devoid of an intrinsic nature is the existence of the reason; for there is not a single thing in the world which is devoid of an intrinsic nature and [at the same time] existent.***

109. 1978:54, note 1.
110. 1957:15; 1994:10.
111. 1929:21.
112. 1929:22.
113. *atha hetorastitvaṃ bhāvāsvābhāvyam ity anupapannam / lokeṣu niḥsvabhāvo na hi kaścana vidyate bhāvaḥ // yadi hetorastitvaṃ manyase niḥsvabhāvāḥ sarvabhāvā iti tad anupapannam. . . .*
114. 1978: 105.

If you think that the fact that things are devoid of an intrinsic nature is the existence of the reason [we answer:] that argument is not valid. . . .

According to this interpretation, the point being made here is that we could also not assume that Nāgārjuna's thesis of universal emptiness establishes itself, that is, that the fact that things are without substance itself could be used as a reason. For the opponent will obviously just deny that this reason holds, that is, that there are things without substance. In this way there there will an argumentational deadlock where all each side can do is insist that their position is right.

There is no decisive way of settling which way of interpreting the verse is the right one. The reading presented here has the advantage that it lets the opponent's replies in verses 18 and 19 fall into the now familiar pattern that we recall from verses 1 and 2, that is, the attempt to demonstrate that Nāgārjuna could coherently assume neither the existence nor the non-existence of specific important entities. In the previous verses the opponent applied this argument to the statement of Nāgārjuna's thesis of universal emptiness; here he applies it to any reason Nāgārjuna could give when attempting to prove his thesis in the standard Nyāya framework of logical inference. Bhattacharya's reading has the advantage that we do not have to assume that the Sanskrit (especially in the commentary) is somewhat irregular. We are just faced with the difficult choice between philosophical and linguistic neatness; I opt for the former but encourage readers to make up their own mind.

REPLY

68. Because the case is the same, the difficulty of the absence of the reason, which was noted in the discussion of the method for refuting the example of the mirage, has already been answered by this.

Now the difficulty of the absence of the reason is to be understood as answered as well by this earlier discussion. This is because the very discussion brought up in the earlier reason of the negation of the set of six is also to be considered here.

This difficulty can be solved by referring to the discussion of the mirage in verses 13–16. Nāgārjuna does not want to accept the suggestion made in verse 18 that a separate reason is not necessary for establishing his thesis of universal emptiness. The negation uttered by the guide, saying that there is no water in the mirage, undoubtedly exists and constitutes the reason why the travelers do not rush toward it to quench their thirst. Yet this negation is as empty as everything else, because it too is dependently originated. But it nevertheless succeeds in removing the mistaken belief of the deluded travelers that water is to be found in front of them. By analogy, the reason Nāgārjuna gives for his thesis of universal emptiness, even though it is empty itself, can function in an argument for his position.

3.9. Negation and Temporal Relations [20, 69]

*20. **Supposing that the negation is earlier, and the negated later fails to be successful. And being later and being simultaneous fail to be successful. Therefore substance exists.***

In the last objection the opponent presents, he considers the temporal relation between the negations and their objects. Even though his worry is phrased in completely general terms, it is primarily directed against the negation contained in Nāgārjuna's thesis of universal emptiness.

In this context, supposing that the negation is earlier and the negated, what is lacking substance, later is not successful. For while there is no object of negation, what is the negation a negation of?

As temporal relations between a negation and the objected negated by it are at issue here, it is most useful to think of negations as particular cognitions produced in the mind when considering a specific object, rather than as the result of applying a negation operator to some propositional content. In the latter case, we would think of the matter in terms of a logical relation between two abstract objects, and as abstract objects do not exist in time, questions regarding their temporal relationship appear ill-formed. The opponent's understanding seems to be modeled better by comparing the operation of negation to the impact of a hammer that causally affects a clay pot (the object of negation) and causes it to break, rather than by understanding it as along the lines of a truth-functional operator being attached to a proposition.[115]

A cognition which is such a negation is obviously existentially dependent on whatever is negated by it, as it cannot exist before this. If we conceive of negation as a cognitive operation performed on a particular mental content, it is evident that there cannot be the negation of a given content as long as the content is not there. This applies to cognitive operations in general; for example, we cannot form a doubt like "Is it raining?" as long as we do not have the mental content the doubt is based on at our disposal.

Moreover, supposing that the negation is later and the object of negation earlier is also not successful. For once the object of negation is established, what does the negation do?

But if we think of negation as a cognitive operation, then what is wrong with the second position, that the object of negation is earlier and the negation later,

115. For some remarks on this causal understanding of negation see Mookerjee (1957:16, note 1).

because the negation is the result of the negation operation having been applied to this particular mental content? If we remind ourselves of the kind of semantics the Naiyāyika employs, we realize that this becomes problematic once we set out to negate a simple perception. The Naiyāyika thesis that simple terms are guaranteed to refer is based on the epistemological claim that the simple perceptions such terms express cannot be erroneous. In the same way as empty terms exclusively arise by putting together referring terms in an illicit way, errors arise exclusively from judgments, where perceptions are put together in an illicit way, but never from the perceptions themselves. But once we have apprehended something truly by a simple perception, the negation, which denies the existence of that very thing, is necessarily false. It is also pointless, since it can never establish the non-existence of something that has already been validated by perception.

If we suppose that the negation and the object of negation are simultaneous, then the negation is not the cause of the object to be negated and the object of negation is not the cause of the negation. In the same way, considering the two horns of a cow,[116] *which have arisen simultaneously, it is clearly not the case that the right one is the cause of the left or the left the cause of the right.*

Nāgārjuna now turns to the second position, the view that negation and negated object can be simultaneous. Negation is conceived of in causal terms. It appears to be the case that it is an essential part of our concept of causation that the cause is *earlier* than the effect. When things come into existence and go out of existence at the same time, such as the two horns of a cow, we do not regard one as causing another, and indeed it would be hard to justify why we should say the right horn caused the left, rather than the other way round. Even in the case of simultaneous and clearly correlated events, we find it hard to come up with a convincing causal explanation. When a boy and a girl sit on a see-saw, the boy going down is simultaneous and clearly correlated with the girl going up. But we would not want to say that his going down *causes* the girl going up, since we would then have to deny that the girl going up causes the boy to go down, since if A causes B, B does not cause A. But such a denial could not be justified, since if we started from the assumption that the girl going up causes the boy to go down, we would have to deny that the boy going down causes the girl to go up.

116. The Sanskrit manuscript has *goviṣāṇayoḥ* (Yonezawa 2008:248:13), Sāṅkṛtyāyana reconstructed from the Tibetan *ri bong gi rwa* to *śa[śa]viṣāṇayor*. Philosophically, instead of; the former reading is more satisfactory. The Tibetan seems to conflate the example of the two horns of the cow used in the discussion of causation (see; for example; Candrakīrti's *Prasannapadā* 139:14 and 224:4) with that of the horn of a hare, a common example in the discussion of non-existent and impossible objects.

In this context, it is also useful to recall Hume's observation that the simultaneity of cause and effect, being a transitive relation, would have a curious consequence.[117] Since the effect of a cause is generally the cause of a further effect if the first cause and its effect are simultaneous, the effect causing other effects will also be simultaneous with these, so that everything would happen at once and there would be no causal ordering in time.

Therefore, if the causal relation presupposes that its relata are not simultaneous, negation and negated object cannot be simultaneous if they are conceptualized in causal terms.

In this context, the statement "all things are without substance" is not tenable.

Since all the possible temporal relations between the negation and the negated object have now been explored and found to be wanting, the opponent concludes that therefore Nāgārjuna's negation of substance cannot proceed.

The secondary literature sometimes notes the similarity between the opponent's argument in verse 20 and the *Nyāyasūtra* 2.1.8–11, where a criticism of the temporal relation between epistemic instruments and objects along similar lines is discussed.[118] The argument presented there is, however, much closer to verse 12 of the *Vaidalyaprakaraṇa*, where Nāgārjuna addresses this matter explicitly.

More interesting in the present context is the irony of the fact that in his argument against the possibility of negation, the opponent applies the very argument against the possibility of causal relations Nāgārjuna gives in his autocommentary on verse 6 of the *Śūnyatāsaptati*:[119]

> Moreover, a cause is not justified in the three times. Why is this? If it is thought that the cause is prior [to the effect], of what is it the cause? Nevertheless, if it is thought that [the cause] is later [than the effect], then what need is there for a cause, as the effect is already existent? Or else if it is thought that cause and effect are simultaneous, then among the pair of cause and effect that arise at the same time, which is the cause of which and which is the effect of which? Thus, in all the three times, a cause is not justified.

If we think of negation as a causal process along the lines the opponent suggests (there is some mental content to which we apply the cognitive operation of negation, and this causes the cognition of negation in our mind), then it seems as if on Nāgārjuna's own terms his thesis of universal emptiness cannot

117. 1896:I, III, II:76.

118. See Meuthrath (1999: 46–58) for a detailed discussion. See also Āryadeva's *Catuśataka* 13:12 (Dhondhup 2007: 20–21), Rinchen (1994: 257).

119. Lindtner (1982b: 221:16–22), Della Santina (2002: 155). See also Westerhoff (2009a: 113–124).

be justified. This thesis is a negation of substance, and is therefore caused, but since "a cause is not justified in the three times," the thesis presumably cannot be justified either.

REPLY

69. *Because the case is the same, the difficulty of the reason in the three times has already been answered by this. The proponent of emptiness obtains the counter-reason of the three times.*

It has to be understood that the issue of expressing the negation in the three time was answered earlier. Why? Because of the fallacy of the same predicament.[120] *As far as according to your statement the negation is not achieved in the three times, the object of negation is like the negation. While negation and object of negation do not exist, you cannot maintain that "the negation is negated." The very reason of the assertion of the negation of the three times is obtained by the proponents of emptiness, and not by you, since they are negators of the substance of all things.*

It is not quite clear which earlier passage Nāgārjuna has in mind here. There is an obvious similarity with the reply suggested by the opponent in verse 4 ("If I cannot employ negation, then your negation of my negation is impossible as well"). However, the case there is merely hypothetical: Nāgārjuna would have accused the opponent of the fallacy of the same predicament, had he taken this reply on board. In addition, verse 4 also does not mention any problems with negation in connection with temporal relations.

In his reply Nāgārjuna attacks neither the opponent's criticism of causality (which he explicitly endorses elsewhere) nor the assumption that negation is a causal process. Instead, he claims that if the opponent's worries were well-founded, the opponent's negation of Nāgārjuna's thesis of universal emptiness and Nāgārjuna's negation of substance would share the same predicament. For if negation is impossible for Nāgārjuna because of the reasons given in verse 20, the very same problem arises for the opponent trying to negate the thesis of universal emptiness. The object of the opponent's negation, that is, Nāgārjuna's claim of universal emptiness and the opponent's attempted negation of this, share the same properties. Since the opponent's negation is caused, too, and since he claims that causally understood negation cannot be made sense of, his negation cannot be established, either. The opponent just *presupposes* that his

120. As in verse 28, Nāgārjuna uses the term *sādhyasama*. The way it is employed here makes it clear the notion of *sādhyasama* has a considerably wider scope than that of *petitio principii*. Here accusing the opponent of *sādhyasama* is much closer to a *tu quoque* claim (since the opponent's negation would face the very same problems he argues Nāgārjuna's negation to have) or to an accusation of inconsistency (since the opponent's argument from the three times implies difficulties for his own use of negation, but he simultaneously assumes that his use of negation is free from such difficulties).

negation is exempt from the problem he describes and is therefore established as a negation of Nāgārjuna's position. But this establishment is the very thing he has to prove here.

The final sentence makes it clear that the opponent's rejection of negation and causality as existent in the three times is accepted by him for the sake of argument only, since he wants to demonstrate that on this assumption Nāgārjuna's theory runs into the difficulty of being unable to establish its own central tenet. Unlike the opponent, however, Nāgārjuna endorses the criticism of causality referred to in verse 20. As a proponent of emptiness, the reason for the difficulty of asserting negation in the three times, which is precisely the universal emptiness of phenomena, forms an essential part of Nāgārjuna's theory and is not just adopted by him for its argumentative use.

It is interesting to note that Nāgārjuna's move against the opponent, claiming that if he cannot negate substance, his opponent cannot negate his negation of substance, has a close parallel in *Nyāyasūtra* 2.1.12[121] and in Vātsyāyana's commentary on this verse. We recall that the previous four verses of the *Nyāyasūtra* presented an argument that epistemic instrument and objects cannot be connected by the three temporal relations of anteriority, posteriority, or simultaneity. The first reply made there is that if the epistemic instruments and objects cannot exist in the three times, the same applies to negation and its object. The objector has therefore undermined his own ability to negate the epistemic instruments and objects, as his criticism of these comes at the price of incapacitating his own ability to negate anything.

Alternatively it is answered by what was said earlier: "63. ***I do not negate anything, and there is nothing to be negated. To this extent you misrepresent me when you say 'you negate.'"***

Nāgārjuna's second reply takes us back to the discussion of verse 11, where the opponent argued that according to the Nyāya semantics, only referring terms can feature in negations, so that in disagreement with what Nāgārjuna wants to claim, "substance" must be a referring term. Nāgārjuna replied to this by rejecting the Naiyāyika's semantic theory which holds that simple designators in negations can never be empty. Since he does not claim that there is an object in the world to which the term "substance" in the negative statement "all things are without substance" refers, he does not negate anything, because there is no such object the existence of which he negates.

Now the argument against causation to which the opponent appeals in verse 20 and which Nāgārjuna accepts is meant to show that cause and effect

121. "The negation is not accomplished as the three times are not established" *traikālyāsiddheḥ pratiṣedhānupapattiḥ*.

do not exist substantially, that is, that the terms "cause" and "effect" do not pick out two mind-independent objects related by a similarly objective causal relation. Rather, cause and effect are a very fundamental piece of the mind's handiwork, both of which are projected out together in order to organize the world of experiences.[122] The opponent is certainly justified in applying this argument to two particular causal relata, namely, negation and its object. In doing so he can infer that these two are empty as well, which is exactly what Nāgārjuna's rejection of Nyāya semantics for negative statements amounts to. As he pointed out at various places earlier in the text, this emptiness of negation does not entail that it does not exist or is argumentationally ineffective.

Then you may think "negation is established in the three times as well. The cause is seen at the time before, as well as at the time after, as well as at the same time. In this case, the cause at the time before is like the father of the son; at the time after, it is like the student of the teacher; and at the same time, it is like the illumination of the lamp."

As a reply, the opponent might now take back his criticism in verse 20 and assert the opposite: that the temporal relations of anteriority, posteriority, and simultaneity do exist between cause and effect and that they also hold between negation and the object of negation. In order to argue for the former, the opponent brings up three examples. The pair father-son represents an obvious example where the existence of the cause precedes the existence of the effect. For the pair student-teacher, we can argue that the student is the cause of the teacher, since as long as he has no students the teacher is no teacher. It is therefore the students who bring about the teacher. At the same time, the teacher (the effect) can have existed before the student and will usually have done so, at the time when he acquired the knowledge he is later to impart. Finally, considering the pair lamp-illumination, it is plain that the former causes the latter but both exist at the very same time. (We should not think here of a lamp which we can switch on and off, and which can therefore exist in an unilluminated state, but rather along the lines of a flame and the illumination it provides.)

We reply: It is not like that. This is because this manner of proceeding contains the three difficulties mentioned earlier.

But these examples do nothing to defuse the worries about the temporal relation of cause and effect presupposed by verse 20, which Nāgārjuna shares. Not only is it impossible to refer to the father as "father" before the son exists, we can also formulate a relatively strong case against him (or at least other causes like him) existing prior to their effects. It often make sense to think of a cause not just in terms of a single entity, like a seed, but as a causal field, incorporating

122. For a more detailed discussion of this matter, see Westerhoff (2009a:91–127).

the water, soil, sunlight and so forth, as well. Furthermore, we might not believe that a property corresponds to any arbitrary collection of objects. But in this case, the property "being the cause of the sprout" does not exist automatically when there is a seed, water, and so forth. It is rather the existence of the seed, the effect, which lets us group these particular phenomena together as related to the seed in a specific manner and thereby brings the corresponding property into existence. If we conceive of causes in this way there are at least some cases where a cause cannot exist prior to the effect.

The opponent's example of the student and the teacher only succeeds in presenting a case of the effect being earlier than the cause if we assume that the effect is not substantially an effect. For when we say that the teacher, the effect, existed before the student, the cause, we do not say that this very man existed before the student, just that at that time he could not have been called "teacher." But then "being a teacher" or "being an effect of the student" is a property that is not part of his intrinsic nature, as it is a property that the man can have at one time and fail to have at another. If it was part of his nature, and if he therefore did not ever fail to have this property, this has the curious consequence that before the student was born there was an effect without a cause. Neither of these results should be acceptable to the opponent, who wants to defend a realist conception of causation.

The difficulty of the simultaneous existence of cause and effect has been discussed above. It leads to the problem that it does not let us differentiate between cause and effect in terms of temporal sequence, which appears to be an essential part of what we mean when we talk of causation.

Moreover, if you arrive in this way at the existence of the negation, your thesis is abandoned. The negation of substance is established by this method.

On the other hand, if the opponent does not accept Nāgārjuna's criticism of the temporal relations between cause and effect, the original argument presented in verse 20 does not work anymore. As by the opponent's own assertion there is now no problem with causation, and therefore no problem with negation causally conceived, the opponent cannot criticize Nāgārjuna's negation of the substance of all things on these grounds.

3.10. Conclusion [70]

70. For whom there is emptiness, there are all things. For whom there is no emptiness there is nothing whatsoever.

The final verse of the *Vigrahavyāvartanī* does not contain any more replies to the opponent's objections, but fulfills two main functions. First, it links back the *Vigrahavyāvartanī* to the *Mūlamadhyamakakārikā* by alluding to several of its key passages. Second, and more important, it stresses the central point (which Nāgārjuna's develops in detail in chapter 24 of the *Mūlamadhyamakakārikā*) that the thesis of universal emptiness does not annihilate the world of conventions, and in particular that it does not annihilate the stages of the Buddhist path. Not only is emptiness compatible with this path, in fact it is the very precondition of its possibility.

Verse 70 has a close parallel in *Mūlamadhyamakakārikā* 24:14:

> Everything is clear for whom emptiness is clear. Nothing is clear for whom the empty is not clear.[123]

Candrakīrti's commentary on this verse in the *Prasannapadā* follows Nāgārjuna's explication of verse 70 very closely.[124] Both focus on the idea that the theory of emptiness understood as dependent origination provides the basis of central elements of the Buddhist teaching and the way to liberation.

For whom there is emptiness there are all natural and supernatural things. Why? For whom there is emptiness there is dependent origination. For whom there is dependent origination there are the four noble truths. For whom there are the four noble truths there are the fruits of religious practice, and all the special attainments.[125] *For whom there are all the special attainments there are the three jewels, the Buddha, the Dharma, and the Sangha.*

For whom there is dependent origination there is righteousness, its cause and its result, as well as unrighteousness, its cause and its result. For whom there is the righteous and the unrighteous, their cause and their result there are the obscurations, their origin, and their bases.

For whom there is all this, the law of the fortunate and unfortunate states of rebirth, the attainment of the fortunate and unfortunate states of rebirth, the way of going toward the fortunate and unfortunate states of rebirth, the passing beyond the fortunate and unfortunate states of rebirth, the means for passing beyond the fortunate and unfortunate states of rebirth as well as all worldly conventions are established.

That emptiness is to be understood in terms of dependent origination has been stressed frequently by Nāgārjuna. Understood in this way, it provides a natural foundation for the key concepts of the Buddhist doctrine. When the four noble truths describe suffering, its origin, its cessation, and the path leading to this cessation, they describe it as dependently originated. In fact, only because suffering is originated in this way it is possible to bring about its cessation.

123. *sarvaṃ ca yujyate tasya śūnyatā yasya yujyate / sarvaṃ na yujyate tasya śūnyaṃ yasya na yujyate*
124. La Vallée Poussin (1903–1913:500–501), May (1959:234–236).
125. *viśeṣādhigama*. See Edgerton (1953) s.v., May (1959:235, 828).

Were suffering to exist substantially and thereby independent of causes and conditions, no sort of practice, Buddhist or otherwise, could affect it and lead to its ending.[126] Far from annihilating the crucial elements of the Buddhist path, emptiness understood as dependent arising provides the conceptual framework in which these must be understood.

Depending on the accomplishment of the fourth noble truth, that of the path leading to the cessation of suffering, the results of this path come about, and eventually Buddhahood is obtained. In dependence on the Buddha his teaching (the dharma) and those who follow this teaching (the sangha) will arise. We find the negative version of this chain of dependencies described in chapter 24 of the *Mūlamadhyamakakārikā*: If things were not empty there would be no dependent origination; if there was no dependent origination there would be no suffering.[127] If there was suffering which was not dependently arisen and therefore existed substantially, there could not be its arising, cessation, and the path leading to it.[128] If there were no four noble truths, there would be no sangha, no dharma, and no Buddha.[129]

Dependent origination also provides the conceptual basis of the notion of karma, since righteous actions bring about fortunate results, and unrighteous actions bring about misfortune. The more familiar worldly conventions, such as language, laws, and customs, are similarly to be understood as producing further frameworks in which specific actions have specific effects. As the theory of emptiness makes clear, however, these frameworks are not a reflection of some underlying reality. The laws of karma do not flow from the fact that certain actions are intrinsically good or evil; it is rather the fact that specific actions are connected with specific results which makes us ascribe the respective ethical qualities to them. As became clear in the previous discussion, the conventions of language should similarly not be understood as mirroring the structure of a mind-independent reality that exists independent of human interests and concerns.

Nāgārjuna's theory of emptiness therefore advises us, on the one hand, on the best way of according with the dependencies of conventional truth we are bound by, such as the laws of karma; on the other hand, it describes a way in which these conventions can be transcended in order to free ourselves from them.

It is to be understood by each one for himself according to this instruction; only some of it can be taught verbally.

126. *Mūlamadhyamakakārikā* 24:20, 25.
127. 24:20–21.
128. 24:23–25.
129. 24:28–30.

It is not necessary to understand this passage as referring to emptiness as some kind of noumenal reality beyond the grasp of concepts, an interpretation that I also do not think to be very helpful in understanding Nāgārjuna's position in general. All we have to assume Nāgārjuna to say here is that there is a difference between an intellectual understanding of the theory of emptiness and its realization. Put briefly, this difference arises from the fact that substance is regarded as a mistaken superimposition that is projected onto a world which in fact lacks it. While the intellectual understanding of the theory of emptiness can show us why it is mistaken, it cannot in itself remove the superimposition. Even if we follow Nāgārjuna's arguments and agree that there are no substances, this does not imply that substances will no longer appear to us. Their disappearance is nothing that can be brought about by verbal instruction; it is a conceptual shift that each one has to bring about for himself by means of the respective contemplative practices.

Once more:

I venerate the one who taught emptiness, dependent origination, and the Middle Way as one thing, the incomparable Buddha.

In these final lines of the *Vigrahavyāvartanī*, Nāgārjuna echoes the praise of the Buddha which opens the *Mūlamadhyamakakārikā* ("I venerate the perfect Buddha, the best of speakers, who taught dependent origination and the auspicious cessation of conceptual constructions")[130] and fuses this praise with one of the most profound verses of the *Mūlamadhyamakakārikā*:

> Whatever is dependently originated, that is declared to be emptiness.
> Being a dependent designation it is itself the Middle Way.[131]

Nāgārjuna stresses once more the identity of the two central concepts, emptiness and dependent arising, which are in turn equated with the Middle Way, the aim of his entire philosophical enterprise. In *Mūlamadhyamakakārikā* 24:18 he equates these with yet another notion, that of dependent designation in order to stress in particular those kinds of dependent origination which are dependencies on verbal conventions. What Nāgārjuna means by adopting a middle way regarding emptiness is that while he does assert its existence, emptiness is not regarded as substantially existent. It is itself a dependently arisen phenomenon which arises in dependence on the erroneous superimposition of substance on phenomena. Emptiness is therefore empty, as well. To tread a middle way with regard to dependent origination is to claim that

130. *yaḥ pratītyasamutpādaṃ prapañcopaśamaṃ śivam / deśayāmāsa saṃbhuddhas taṃ vande vadatāṃ varam.*

131. Mūlamadhyamakakārikā 24:18 *yaḥ pratītyasamutpādaḥ śūnyatāṃ tāṃ pracakṣmahe / sā prajñaptir upādāya pratipat saiva madhyamā.* See Garfield (1995: 304–308).

while all phenomena are dependently arisen and therefore do not exist from their own side, their empty existence does not entail their non-existence. They constitute conventional reality and serve as the ground of conventional truth, a truth which even though not absolute is a truth nevertheless.

This is the end of the verses of the Venerable Nāgārjuna, who composed the 450 verses. It was written down by the noble Dharmakīrti in the way he obtained it, for the sake of all sentient beings.

How to understand the first part of the colophon[132] is not quite clear. But given that the *Mūlamadhyamakakārikā* consists of 448 verses in twenty-seven chapters, plus two verses in the dedication, it appears plausible that the scribe wanted to identify Nāgārjuna as the author of the *Mūlamadhyamakakārikā*, thereby linking back the *Vigrahavyāvartanī* to the main text, the contents of which it sets out to elucidate.

132. *kṛtir iyam ācāryanāgārjunapādān(ā) +++++ ekatra ślokaśata* 450.

Bibliography

Allen, William Sidney. 1953. *Phonetics in Ancient India*. London, Oxford University Press.

Arnold, Dan. 2005. *Buddhists, Brahmins, and Belief: Epistemology in South Asian Philosophy of Religion*. New York, Columbia University Press.

Bhattacharya, Kamaleswar. 1974. "A note on the interpretation of the term *sādhyasama* in Madhyamaka contexts." *Journal of Indian Philosophy* 2:225–230.

———. 1977. "On the relationship between the Vigrahavyāvartanī and the Nyāyasūtras." *Journal of Indo-European Studies* 5(2–3):265–273.

Bhattacharya, Kamaleswar, Elgin H. Johnston, and Arnold Kunst. 1978. *The Dialectical Method of Nāgārjuna*. Second revised and enlarged edition. Delhi, Motilal Banarsidass.

Bodhi, Bikkhu, editor. 2000. *The Connected Discourses of the Buddha*. Boston, Wisdom.

Boghossian, Paul. 2006. *Fear of Knowledge: Against Relativism and Constructivism*. Oxford, Oxford University Press.

Bronkhorst, Johannes. 1985. "Nāgārjuna and the Naiyāyikas." *Journal of Indian Philosophy* 13:107–132.

Burton, David. 1999. *Emptiness Appraised: A Critical Study of Nāgārjuna's Philosophy*. Richmond, Surrey, Curzon.

Cabezón, José Ignacio. 1992. *A Dose of Emptiness: An Annotated Translation of the sTong thun chen mo of mKhas grub dGe legs dpal bzang*. Delhi, Sri Satguru Publications.

Cabezón, José Ignacio, and Geshe Lobsang Dargyay. 2007. *Freedom from Extremes: Gorampa's "Distinguishing the Views" and the Polemics of Emptiness*. Boston, Wisdom.

Chakrabarty, Debasish. 2003. *Vaiśeṣika-Sūtra of Kaṇāda*. New Delhi, D. K. Printworld.

Chatterjee, Satischandra. 1978. *The Nyāya Theory of Knowledge*. Calcutta, University of Calcutta Press.

Chattopadhyaya, Debiprasad, and Mrinalkanti Gangopadhyaya. 1968. *Nyāya Philosophy: Literal translation of Gautama's Nyāya-sūtra & Vātsyāyana's Bhāṣya along with a free and abridged translation of the Elucidation by Mahāmahopādhyāya Phaṇibhūṣaṇa Tarkavāgīśa*. Calcutta, Indian Studies.

Della Santina, Peter. 2002. *Causality and Emptiness: The Wisdom of Nagarjuna*. Singapore, Buddhist Research Society.

dGe 'dun chos 'phel. No date. "dBu ma'i zab gnad snying bor dril ba'i legs bshad klu sgrub dgongs rgyan zhes bya ba bzhugs so." In *'Jam gling ring pa'i dpa' bo mkhas dbang dge 'dun chos phel gyi gsung 'bum bzhugs* 4:1–80. Lhasa, Zhang kang gyi ling dpe skrun khang.

Dhammajoti, K. L. 2004. *Sarvāstivāda Abhidharma*. Second edition. Centre for Buddhist Studies.

Dhondup, Phuntsok (ed.). 2007. *bZhi brgya pa'i rnam bshad legs bshad snying po. The Essence of Elegant Sayings: A Comprehensive Commentary on the 400 Verses on Madhyamaka of Acārya Āryadeva by Gyaltsap Darma Rinchen*. Gelugpa Students' Welfare Committee, GHTS, Sarnath, Varanasi.

Dutt, Nalinaksha. 1934. *The Pañcaviṃśatisāhaṣrikā-Prajñāpāramitā*. London, Luzac.

Dwivedi, V. P. 1916. *Sri Bhardwaja Udyotakara: Nyaya Vartikam*. Benares, Vidya Vilas Press.

Edgerton, Franklin. 1953. *Buddhist Hybrid Sanskrit Grammar and Dictionary*. New Haven, Yale University Press.

Feer, Léon, editor. 1884–1898. *Saṃutta Nikāya*. London, Pali Text Society.

Frauwallner, Erich. 1995. *Studies in Abhidharma Literature and the Origins of Buddhist Philosophical Systems*. Albany, State University of New York Press.

Garfield, Jay. 1995. *The Fundamental Wisdom of the Middle Way: Translation and Commentary of Nāgārjuna's Mūlamadhyamakakārikā*. Oxford, Oxford University Press.

Gautama. *Nyaya-vartikum*. 1887. Edited by Paṇḍit Vindhyeśvarī Prasad Dube. Bibliotheca Indica N.S. 625. Calcutta, Asiatic Society.

Hahn, Michael. 1982. "On a numerical problem in Nāgārjuna's *Ratnāvali*." In *Indological and Buddhist Studies: Volume in Honour of Professor J. W. de Jong on His Sixtieth Birthday*, edited by L. A. Hercus et al., 161–185. Canberra, Faculty of Asian Studies, Australian National University.

Halbfass, Wilhelm. 1992. *On Being and What There Is: Classical Vaiśeṣika and the History of Indian Ontology*. Delhi, Sri Satguru Publications.

Hiraga, Yumiko, et al. 2001. *Introduction to the Facsimile Edition of a Collection of Sanskrit Palm-leaf Manuscripts in Tibetan dBu med script*. Tokyo, Study Group of Sanskrit Manuscripts in Tibetan *dBu med* script, Institute for Comprehensive Studies of Buddhism, Taishō University.

Hume, David. 1896. *A Treatise of Human Nature*. Oxford, Clarendon Press.

Jha, Gaṅgānātha. 1984. *Nyāyadarśanam with Vātsyāyana's Bhāṣya, Uddyotakara's Vārtika, Vācaspati Miśra's Tātparyaṭīkā and Viśvanātha's Vṛtti*. Delhi, Motilal Banarsidass.

Jhalakīkar, Mahāmahopādyāya Bhīmācārya. 1996. *Nyāyakośa or Dictionary of Technical Terms of Indian Philosophy*. Fourth edition. Pune, Bhandarkar Oriental Research Institute.

Johnston, Elgin H. 1938. "Nāgārjuna's list of *kuśaladharmas*." *Indian Historical Quarterly* 14:314–323.

Johnston, Mark. 1996. "Better than mere knowledge? The function of sensory awareness." In Tamar Gendler and John Hawthorne, editors, *Perceptual Experience*, 260–290. Oxford, Oxford University Press.

Kajiyama, Yuichi. 1965. "The Vaidalyaprakaraṇa of Nāgārjuna." *Indogaku Shiron Shū*, 6–7:129–155.

Kasawara, Kenjiu, F. Max Müller, and H. Wenzel. 1885. *The Dharma-samgraha: An Ancient Collection of Buddhist Technical Terms*. Oxford, Clarendon Press.

Kielhorn, Franz, editor. 1880–1885. *The Vyākaraṇa-Mahābhāṣya of Patañjali*. Bombay, Government Central Book Depot.

La Vallée Poussin, Louis de, editor. 1912. *Madhyamakāvatāra of Candrakīrti*. St. Petersburg, Académie Impériale des Sciences.

——— editor. 1903–1913. *Mūlamadhyamakakārikās de Nāgārjuna avec la Prasannapadā commentaire de Candrakīrti*. Delhi, Motilal Banarsidass.

———. 1988–1990. *Abhidharmakośabhāṣyam*. English translation by Leo M. Pruden. Berkeley, Asian Humanities Press.

Lamotte, Etienne. 1944–. *La traité de la grande vertu de sagesse*. Louvain, Bureau du Muséon.

Lindtner, Christian. 1982a. *Nagarjuniana: Studies in the Writings and Philosophy of Nāgārjuna*. Copenhagen, Akademisk Forlag.

———. 1982b. *Nāgārjuna's Filosofiske Værker*. Copenhagen, Akademisk Forlag.

Loizzo, Joseph John. 2007. *Nāgārjuna's Reason Sixty with Chandrakīrti's Reason Sixty Commentary*. New York, American Insitute of Buddhist Studies.

Lopez, Donald. 1994. "dGe 'dun Chos 'phel's position on Vigrahavyāvartanī 29." In Tadeusz Skorupski and Ulrich Pagel, editors, *Buddhist Forum* 3:161–185. London, School of Oriental and African Studies.

———. 2005. *The Madman's Middle Way: Reflections on Reality of the Tibetan Monk Gendun Chopel*. Chicago, Chicago University Press.

Mabbett, Ian. 1996. "Is there a Devadatta in the house? Nāgārjuna's Vigrahavyāvartanī and the liar paradox." *Journal of Indian Philosophy* 24:295–320.

Matilal, Bimal. 1968. *The Navya-Nyāya Doctrine of Negation*. Cambridge, Harvard University Press.

———. 1974. "A note on the Nyāya fallacy *sādhyasama* and *petitio principii*." *Journal of Indian Philosophy* 2:211–224.

———. 1986. *Perception: An Essay on Classical Indian Theories of Knowledge*. Oxford, Clarendon.

———. 1987. Review of Kamaleswar Bhattacharya, "The Dialectical Method of Nāgārjuna." *Bulletin of the School of Oriental and African Studies* 45(1):186–187.

May, Jacques. 1959. *Prasannapadā Madhyamakavrtti: Douze chapitres traduits du sanscrit et du tibétain.* Paris, Adrien-Maisonneuve.

Meuthrath, Annette. 1999. *Die Nāgārjuna zugeschriebene Vigrahavyavartanī und die Nyāyasūtras: Eine Untersuchung des Verhältnisses beider Texte zueinander.* Reinbek, Verlag für Orientalische Fachpublikationen.

Miyamoto, K. 1999. "A newly revised Chinese version of the *Vigrahavyāvartanī.*" *Transactions of Kokugakuin University* 37:73–99.

mKhas grub dGe legs dpal bzang. 1983. "sTong thun chen mo." In *Collected Works of mKhas grub dGe legs dpal bzang*, volume *ka*. New Delhi, Ngawang Geleg Demo.

Mookerjee, Satkari. 1957. "The absolutist's standpoint in logic." In Satkari Mookerjee, editor, *The Nava-Nalanda-Mahavihara Research Publication* 1:1–175. Calcutta, Calcutta Private Press.

———. 1994. *Vigrahavyavartani of Acharya Nagarjuna with His Own Commentary.* Varanasi, Bauddha Bharati.

Nagel, Thomas. 1997. *The Last Word.* Oxford, Oxford University Press.

Nakamura, Hajime. 1987. *Indian Buddhism: A Survey with Bibliographical Notes.* Delhi, Motilal Banarsidass.

Nanjio, Bunyiu. 1923. *The Laṅkāvatārasūtra.* Kyoto, Otani University Press.

Napper, Elizabeth. 1989. *Dependent-Arising and Emptiness.* London, Wisdom.

Oberhammer, Gerhard. 1963. "Ein Beitrag zu den Vāda-Traditionen Indiens." *Wiener Zeitschrift für die Kunde Süd- und Ostasiens und Archiv für indische Philosophie* 7:63–103.

Oetke, Claus. 1991. *Zur Methode und Analyse philosophischer Sūtratexte: Die Pramāṇapassagen der Nyāyasūtren.* Reinbek, Verlag für Orientalistische Fachpublikationen.

Potter, Michael. 1990. *Sets: An Introduction.* Oxford, Oxford University Press.

Raghavan, V. 1956. *Yantras or Mechanical Contrivances in Ancient India.* Bangalore, Indian Institute of Culture.

Rahula, Walpola, and Sara Boin-Webb. 2000. *Abhidharmasamuccaya: The Compendium of Higher Teaching.* Fremont, Cal., Asian Humanities Press.

Reat, N. Ross. 1993. *The Śālistamba Sūtra: Tibetan Original, Sanskrit Reconstruction, English Translation, Critical Notes (Including Pāli parallels, Chinese Version and Ancient Tibetan Fragments).* Delhi, Motilal Banarsidass.

Rinchen, Sonam. 1994. *Yogic Deeds of Bodhisattvas: Gyel-tsap on Āryadeva's Four Hundred.* Ithaca, N.Y., Snow Lion.

Ruben, Walter. 1928. *Gautama: Die Nyāyasūtra's.* Leipzig, Abhandlungen für die Kunde des Morgenlandes 18:2.

Ruegg, David Seyfort. 1981. *The Literature of the Madhyamaka School of Philosophy in India.* Wiesbaden, Harrassowitz.

———. 1983. "On the thesis and assertion in Madhyamaka/dBu ma." In Ernst Steinkellner and Helmut Tauscher, editors, *Contributions on Tibetan and Buddhist*

Religion and Philosophy, 205–241. Vienna, Arbeitskreis für Tibetische und Buddhistische Studien.

———. 1986. "Does the Mādhyamika have a thesis and philosophical position?" In Bimal Krishna Matilal, editor, *Buddhist Logic and Epistemology*, 229–237. Dordrecht, D. Reidel.

———. 2000. *Three Studies in the History of Indian and Tibetan Madhyamaka Philosophy*. Vienna, Arbeitskreis für Tibetische und Buddhistische Studien.

———. 2002. *Two Prolegomena to Madhyamaka Philosophy*. Vienna, Arbeitskreis für Tibetische und Buddhistische Studien.

Sagal, Paul T. 1992. "Nagarjuna's paradox." *American Philosophical Quarterly* 29(1):79–85.

Śāstrī, K. Sāmbaśiva. 1926. *The Mīmāmsāṣlokavārtika*. Trivandrum, Government Press.

Sāṇkṛtyāyana, Rāhula. 1935. "Sanskrit palm-leaf manuscripts in Tibet." *Journal of the Bihar and Orissa Research Society* 21:21–43.

———. 1937. "Second search for Sanskrit palm-leaf manuscripts in Tibet." *Journal of the Bihar and Orissa Research Society* 23:1–57.

———. 1938. "Search for Sanskrit MSS. in Tibet." *Journal of the Bihar and Orissa Research Society* 24:137–163.

Schiefner, Antonius. 1868. *Tāranāthae de Doctrinae Buddhicae in India Propagatione Narratio*. St Petersburg, St. Petersburg Academy of Sciences.

Siderits, Mark. 1980. "The Madhyamaka critique of epistemology." *Journal of Indian Philosophy* 8:307–335.

———. 1988. "Nāgārjuna as anti-realist." *Journal of Indian Philosophy* 16:311–325.

———. 2000. "Nyāya realism, Buddhist critique." In Bina Gupta, editor, *The Empirical and the Transcendental*, 219–231. Lanham, MD., Rowman & Littlefield.

———. 2003. *Personal Identity and Buddhist Philosophy*. Aldershot, Ashgate.

———. 2004. "Causation and emptiness in early Madhyamaka." *Journal of Indian Philosophy* 32:393–419.

Steinkellner, Ernst. 2004. *A Tale of Leaves: On Sanskrit Manuscripts in Tibet, Their Past and Their Future*. 2003 Gonda Lecture. Amsterdam, Royal Netherlands Academy of Arts and Sciences.

Stoll, Robert R. 1961. *Set Theory and Its Logic*. New York, Dover.

Tanji, Teruyoshi. 2000. "On Samāropa." In Jonathan Silk, editor, *Wisdom, Compassion, and the Search for Understanding*, 347–368. Honolulu, University of Hawaii Press.

Tillemans, Tom. 2001. "Trying to be fair to Mādhyamika Buddhism." The Numata Yehan Lecture in Buddhism, University of Calgary, Canada.

Tola, Fernando, and Carmen Dragonetti. 1987. "Sūnyatāsaptati: The Seventy Kārikās on Voidness (according to the Svavṛtti) of Nāgārjuna." *Journal of Indian Philosophy* 15:1–55.

———. 1995. *Nāgārjuna's Refutation of Logic*. Delhi, Motilal Banarsidass.

———. 1998. "Against the attribution of the Vigrahavyāvartanī to Nāgārjuna." *Wiener Zeitschrift für die Kunde Südasiens und Archiv für Indische Philosophie* 42:151–166.

Tsong kha pa Blo bzang grags pa. 1985. *Lam rim chen mo*. Qinghai, Tso Ngön (Qinghai) People's Press.

———. 2000–2004. *The Great Treatise on the Stages of the Path to Enlightenment*. Ithaca, N.Y., Snow Lion.

Tucci, Giuseppe. 1929. *Pre-Diṅnāga Buddhist Texts on Logic from Chinese Sources*. Baroda, Gaekwad's Oriental Series.

Warder, A. K. 1980. *Indian Buddhism*. Delhi, Motilal Banarsidass.

Westerhoff, Jan. 2006. "Nāgārjuna's catuṣkoṭi." *Journal of Indian Philosophy* 34:367–395.

———. 2009a. *Nāgārjuna's Madhyamaka: A Philosophical Introduction*. Oxford, Oxford University Press.

———. 2009b. "Making sense of verse 29 of the *Vigrahavyāvartanī*." In Mario D'Amato, Jay Garfield, and Tom Tillemans (eds.), *Pointing at the Moon: Buddhism, Logic, and Analytic Philosophy*. Oxford, Oxford University Press, pp. 25–39.

———. 2010. "The merely conventional existence of the world." In Jay Garfield, Graham Priest, et al. (eds.), *Moonshadows. The Doctrine of the Two Truths from Candrakīrti to the Present*. Oxford, Oxford University Press.

Wogihara, U. 1932–1935. *Abhisamayālaṃkārālokā Prajñāpāramitāvyākhyā*. Tokyo, Toyo Bunko.

Wood, Thomas E. 1994. *Nāgārjunian Disputations: A Philosophical Journey through an Indian Looking-glass*. Honolulu, University of Hawaii Press.

Woodward, F. L. 1979. *The Book of Gradual Sayings (Aṅguttara-Nikāya)*. London, Pali Text Society.

Yamaguchi, Susumu. 1929. "Traité de Nāgārjuna pour écarter les vaines discussions (Vigraha-vyāvartanī)." *Journal Asiatique* 215:3–86.

———. 1949. "Ejōron nitsuite (on the Vigraha-vyāvartanī)." *Mikkyō bunka* 7:1–19.

Yonezawa, Yoshiasu. 1991. "On a text of the Vigrahavyāvartanī." *Journal of Indian and Buddhist Studies* 40(1).

———. 2008. "Vigrahavyāvartanī: Sanskrit transliteration and Tibetan translation." *Journal of Naritasan Institute of Buddhist Studies* 31:209–333.

Index

CPSIA information can be obtained
at www.ICGtesting.com
Printed in the USA
BVHW070020210919
559046BV00003B/59/P

9 780199 732708